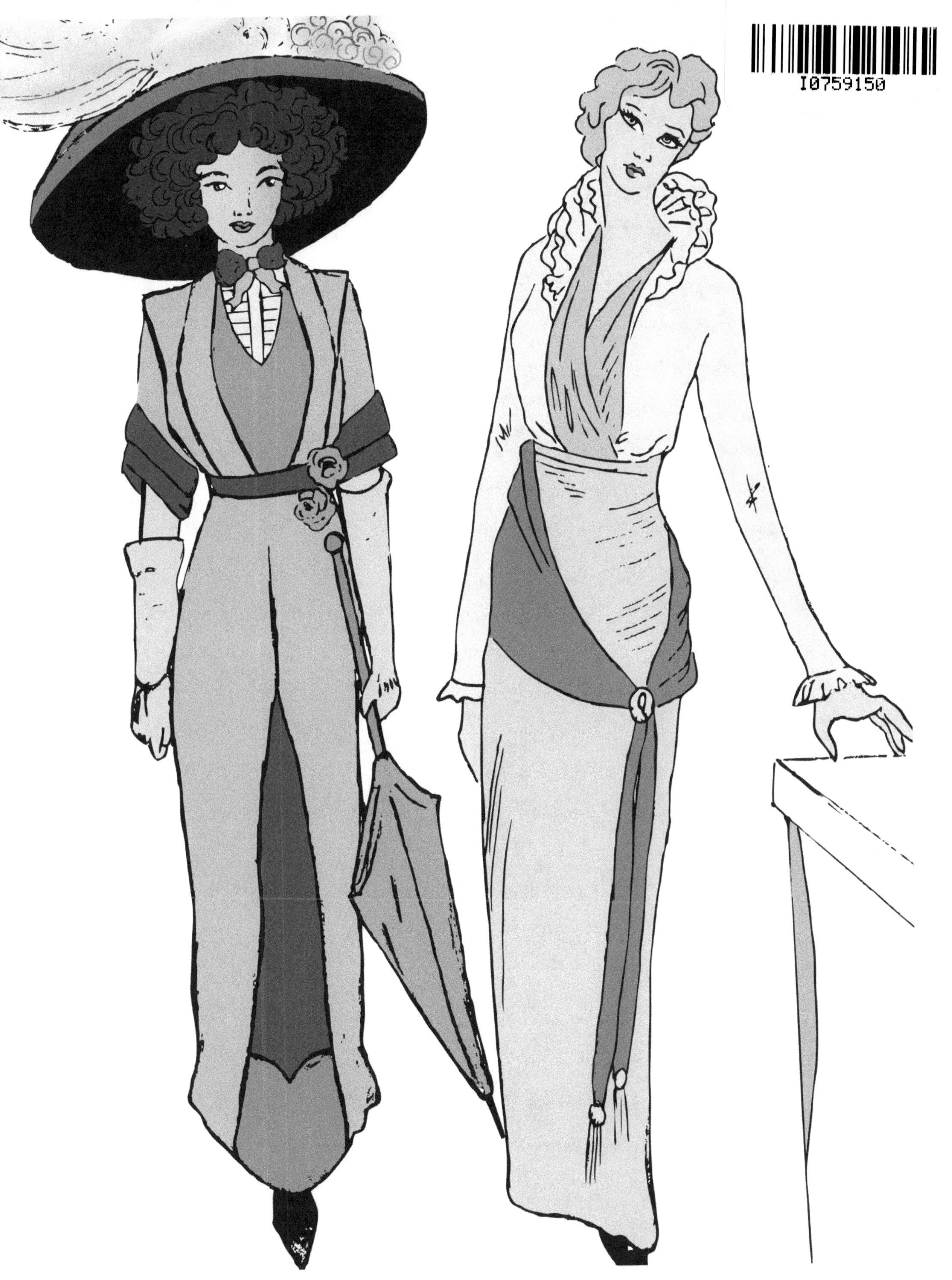

Beautiful Vintage Women To Color

COLORING BOOK

Protect your artwork from bleeding by placing a blank sheet of paper under your work

TEST YOUR MARKERS

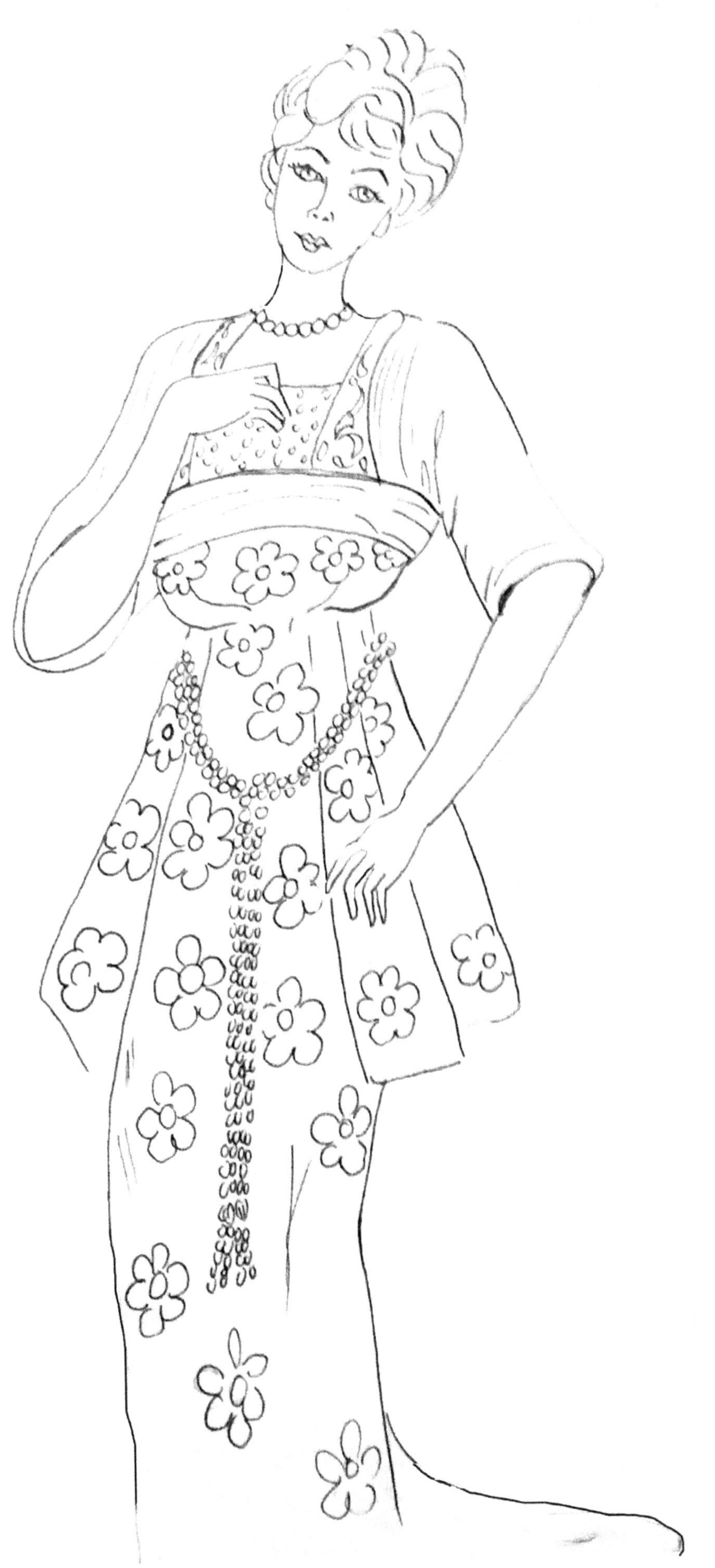

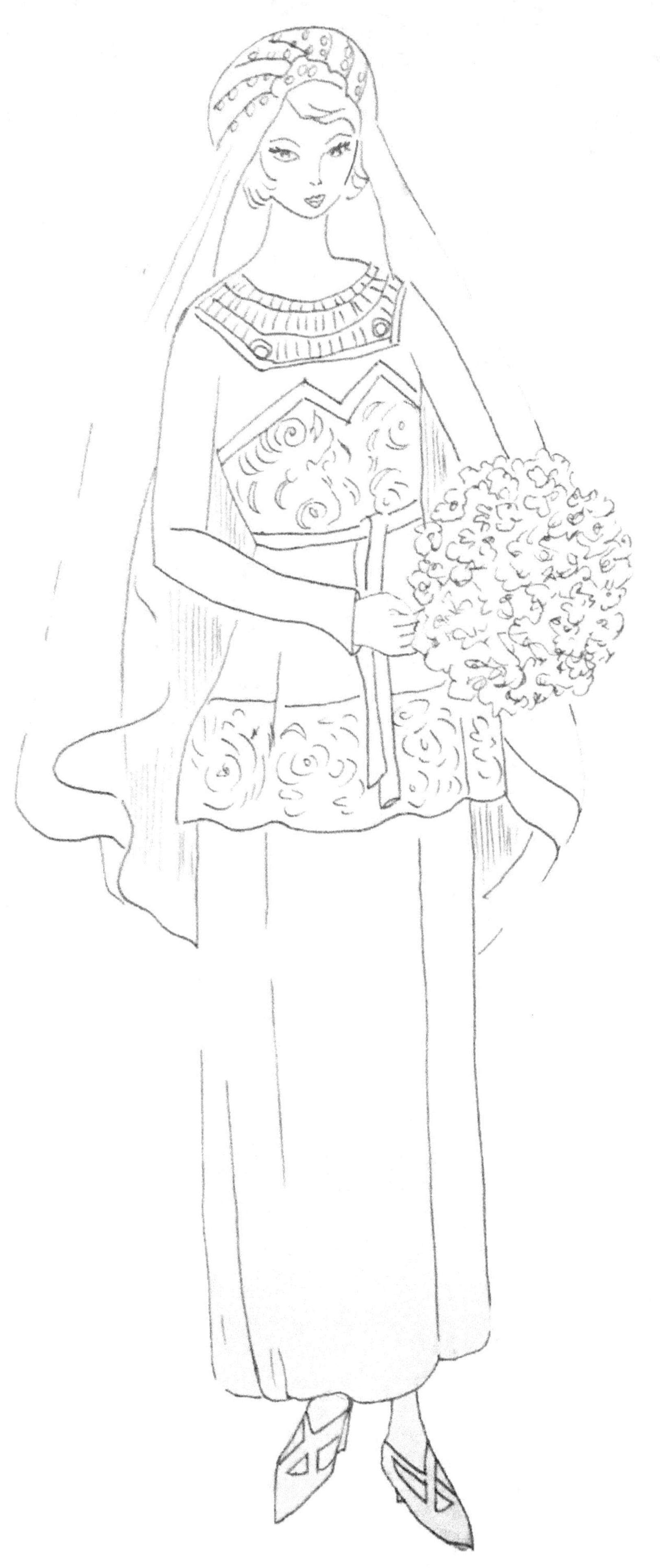

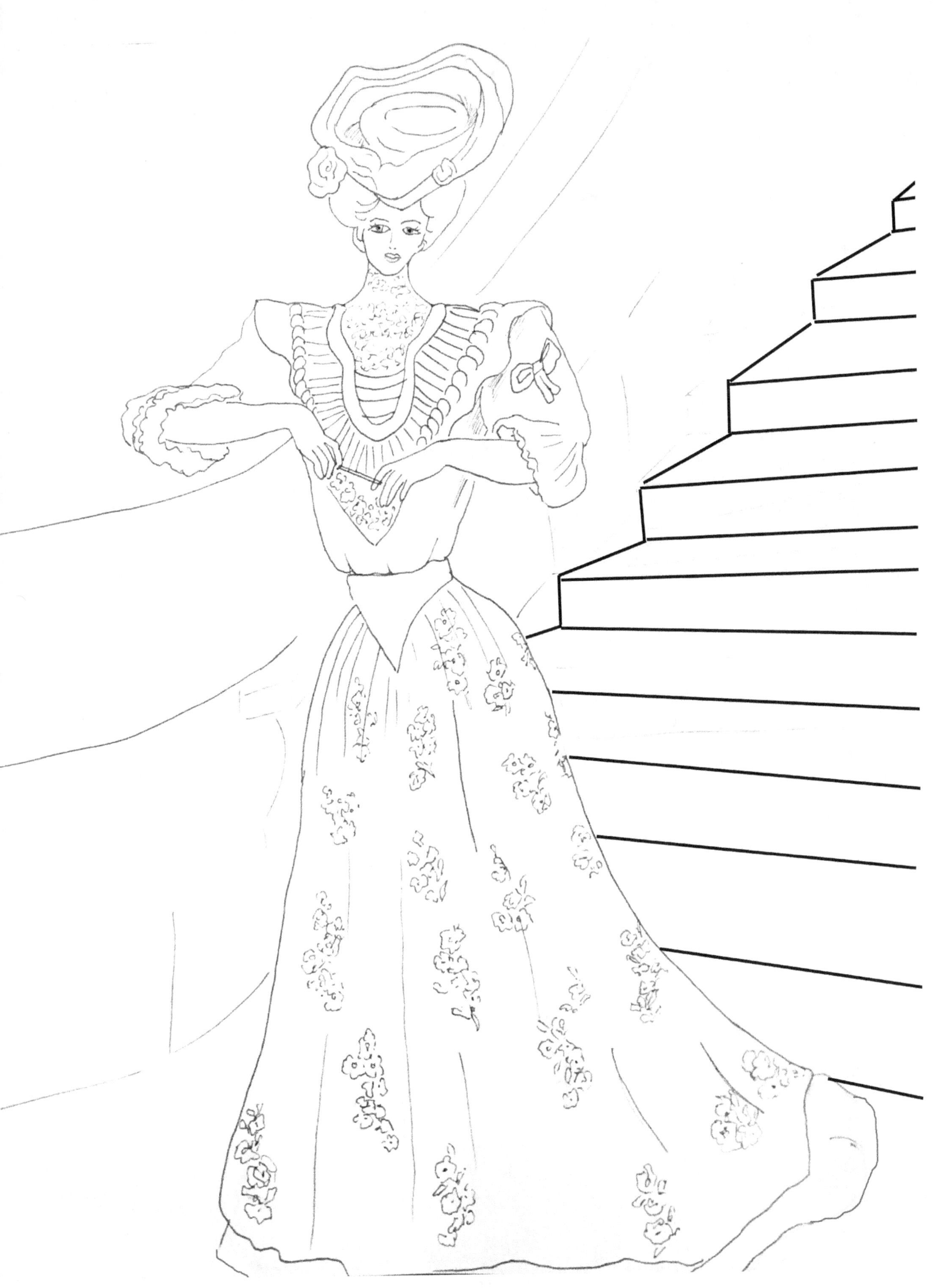

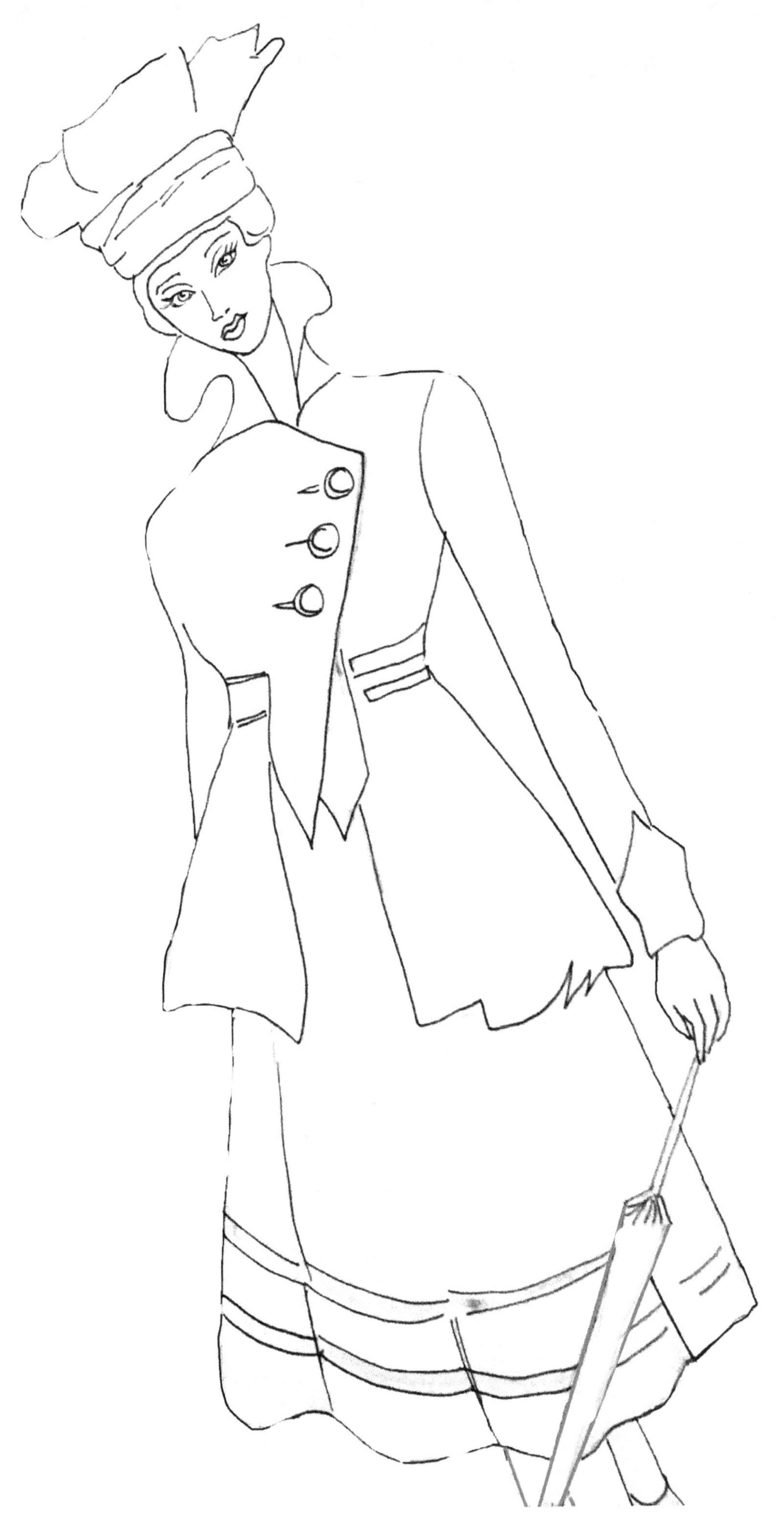

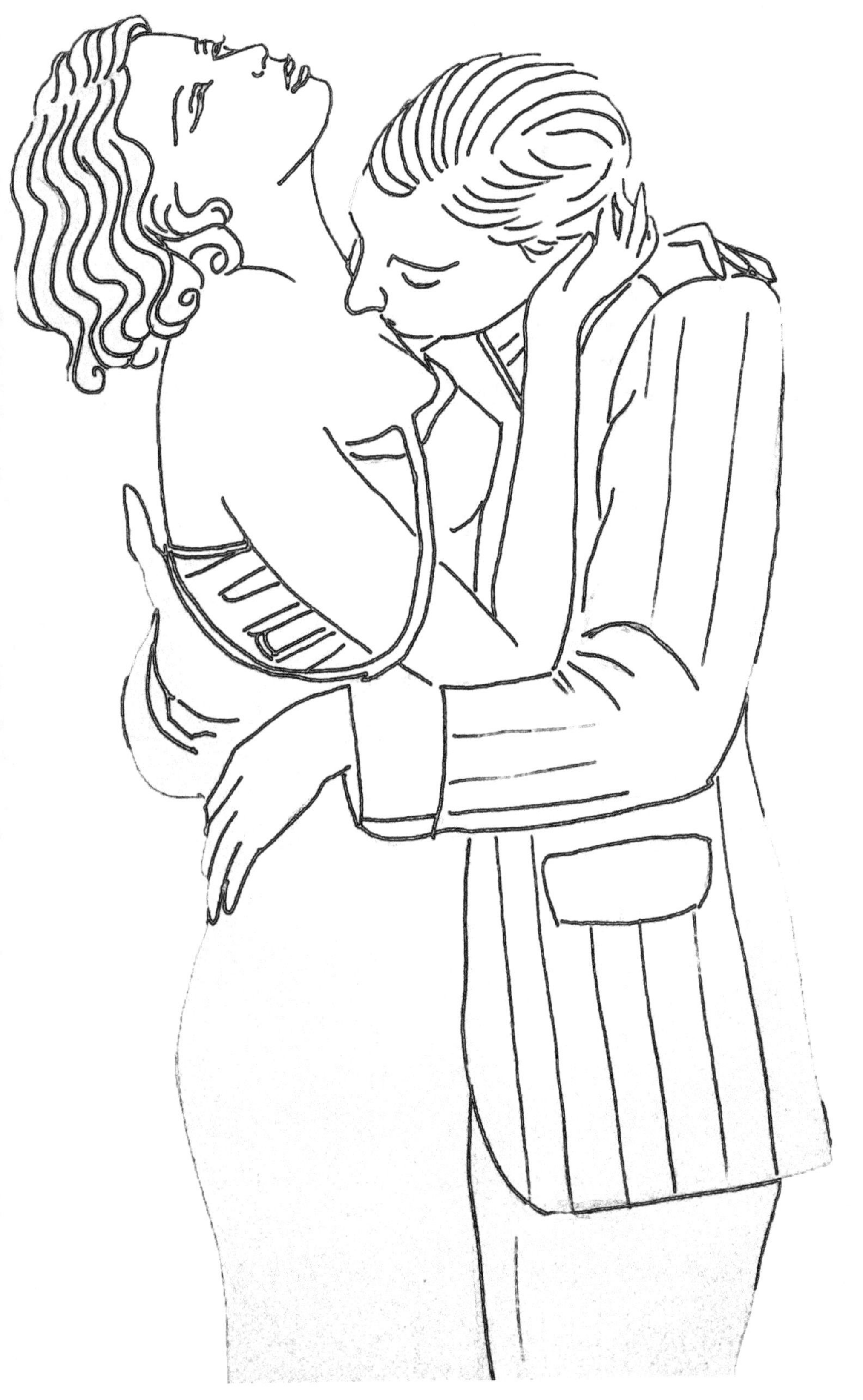

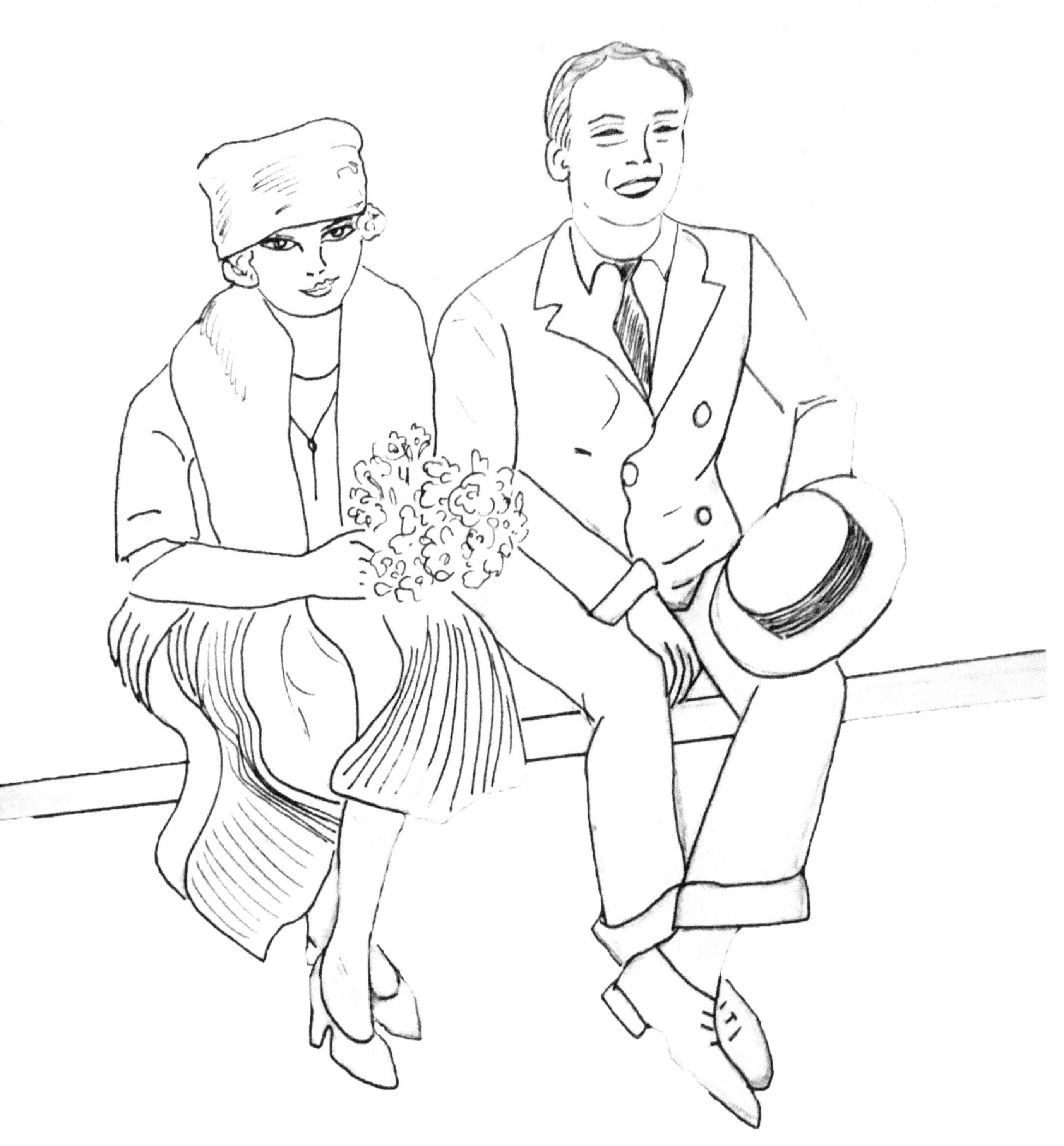

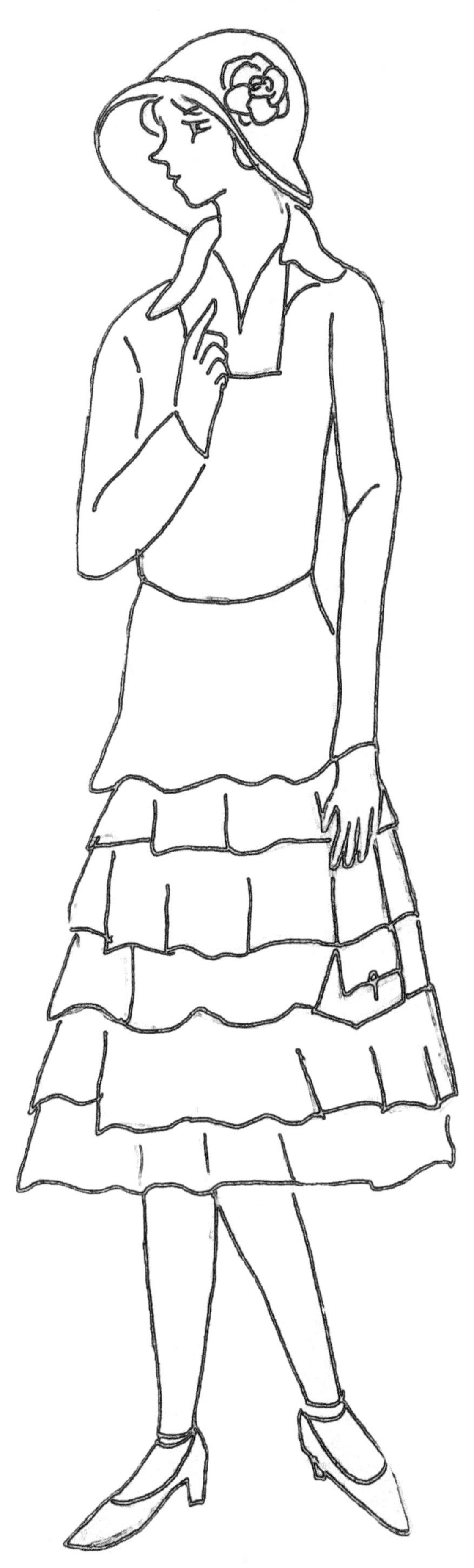

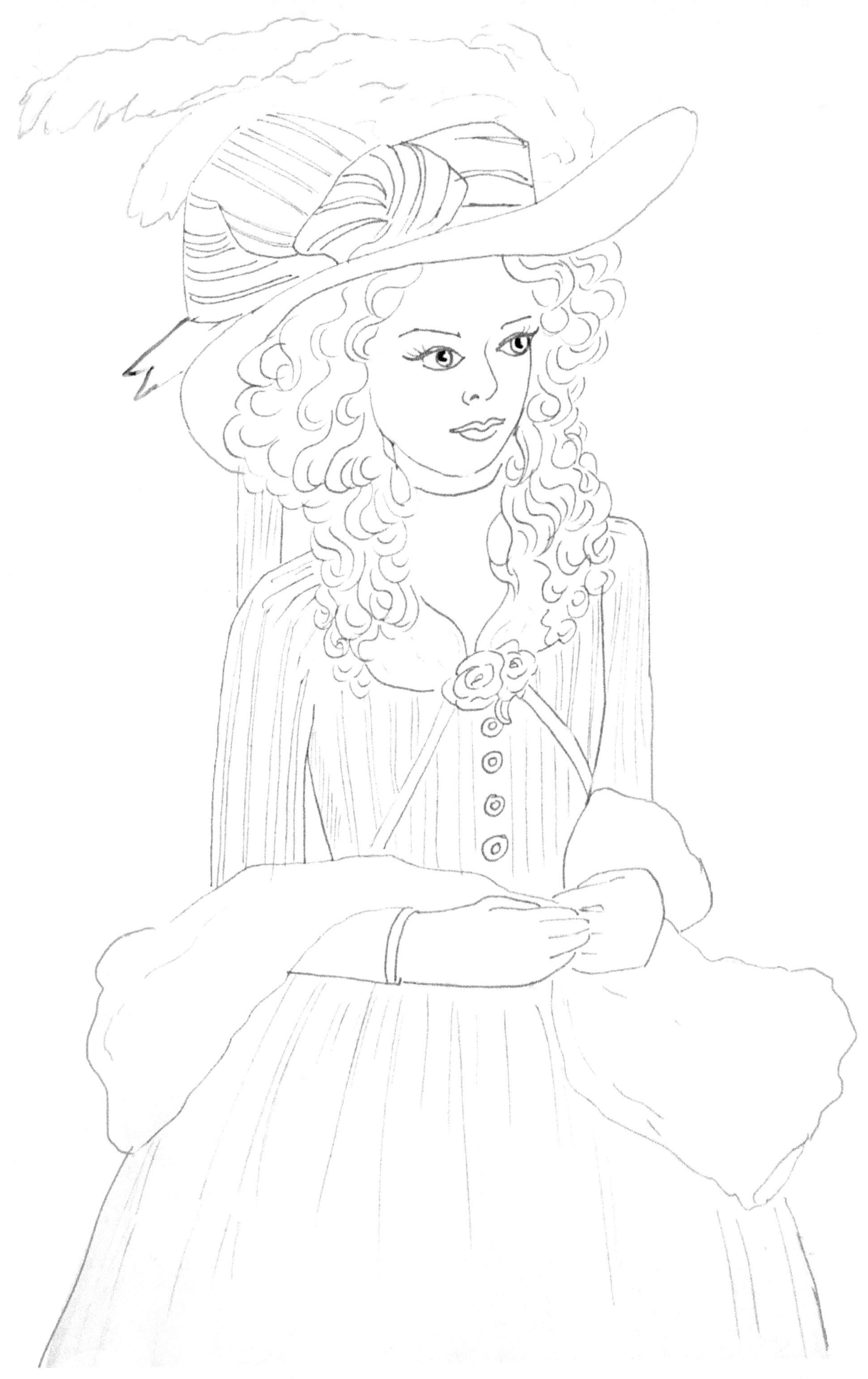

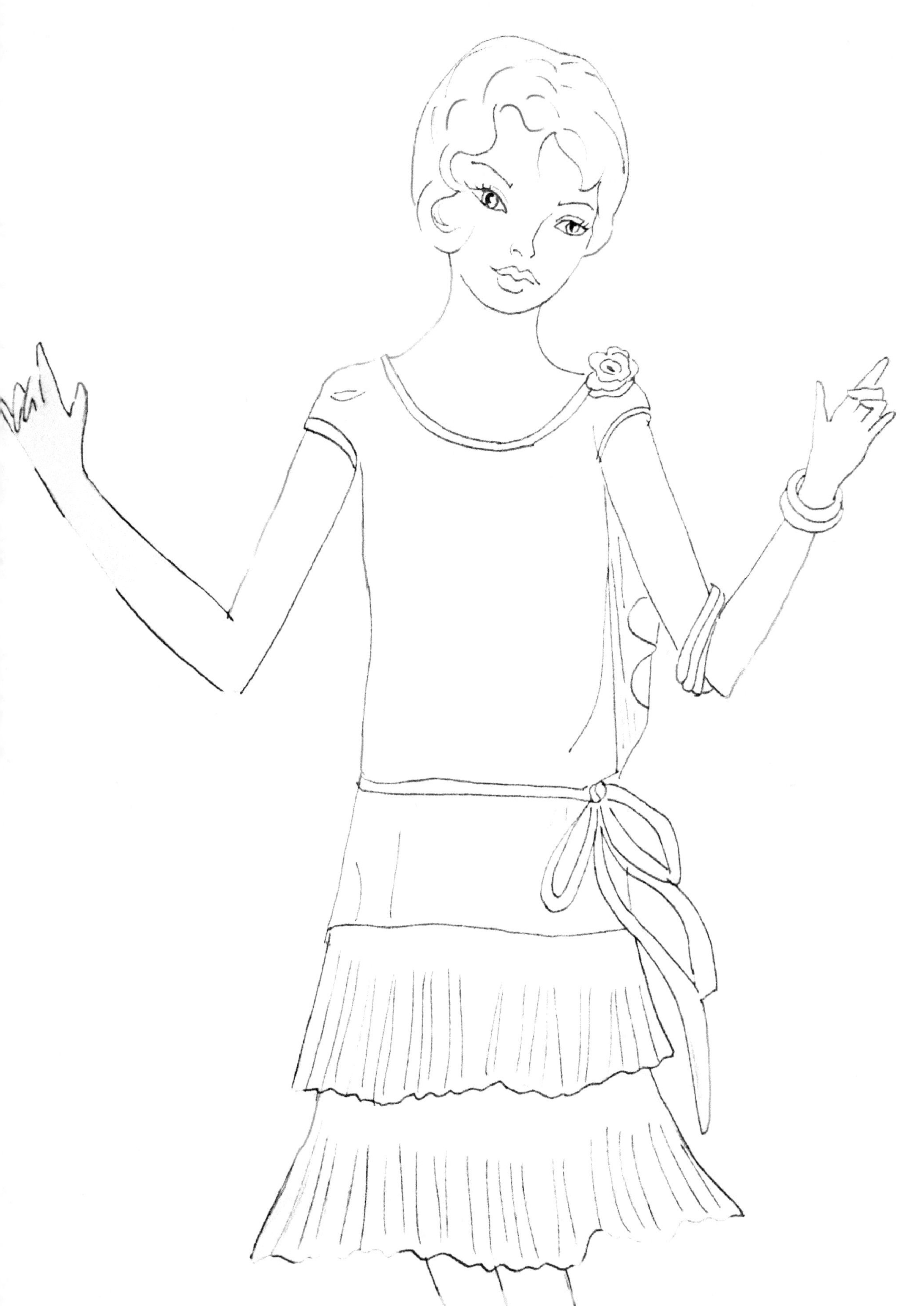

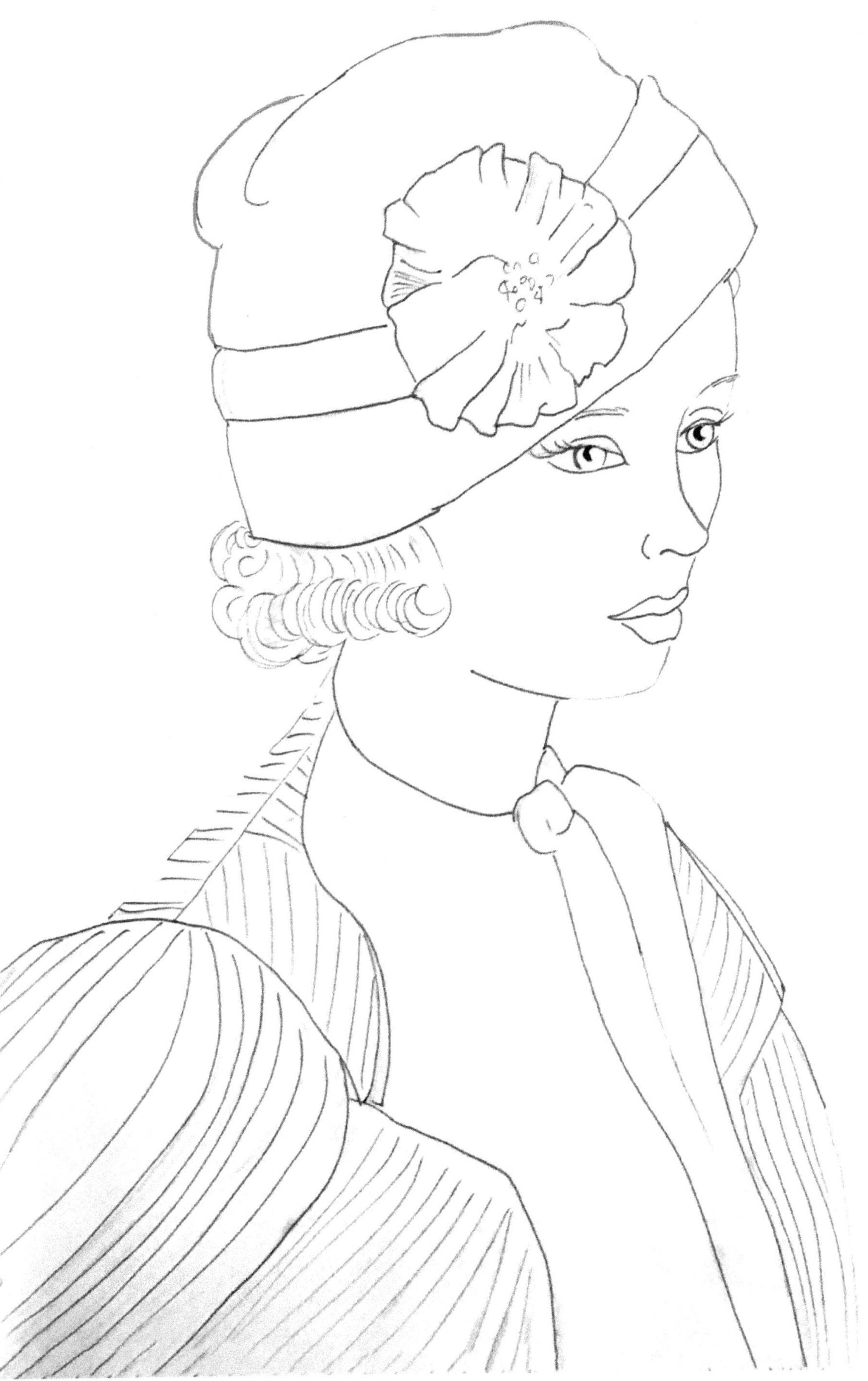

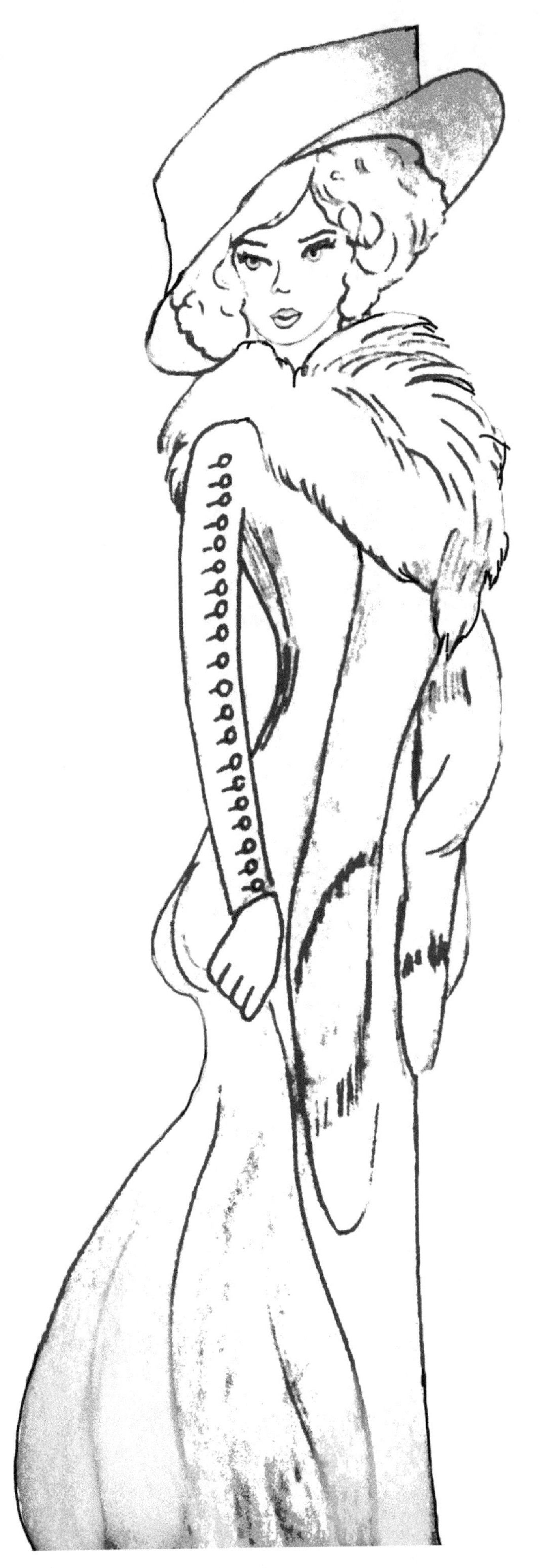

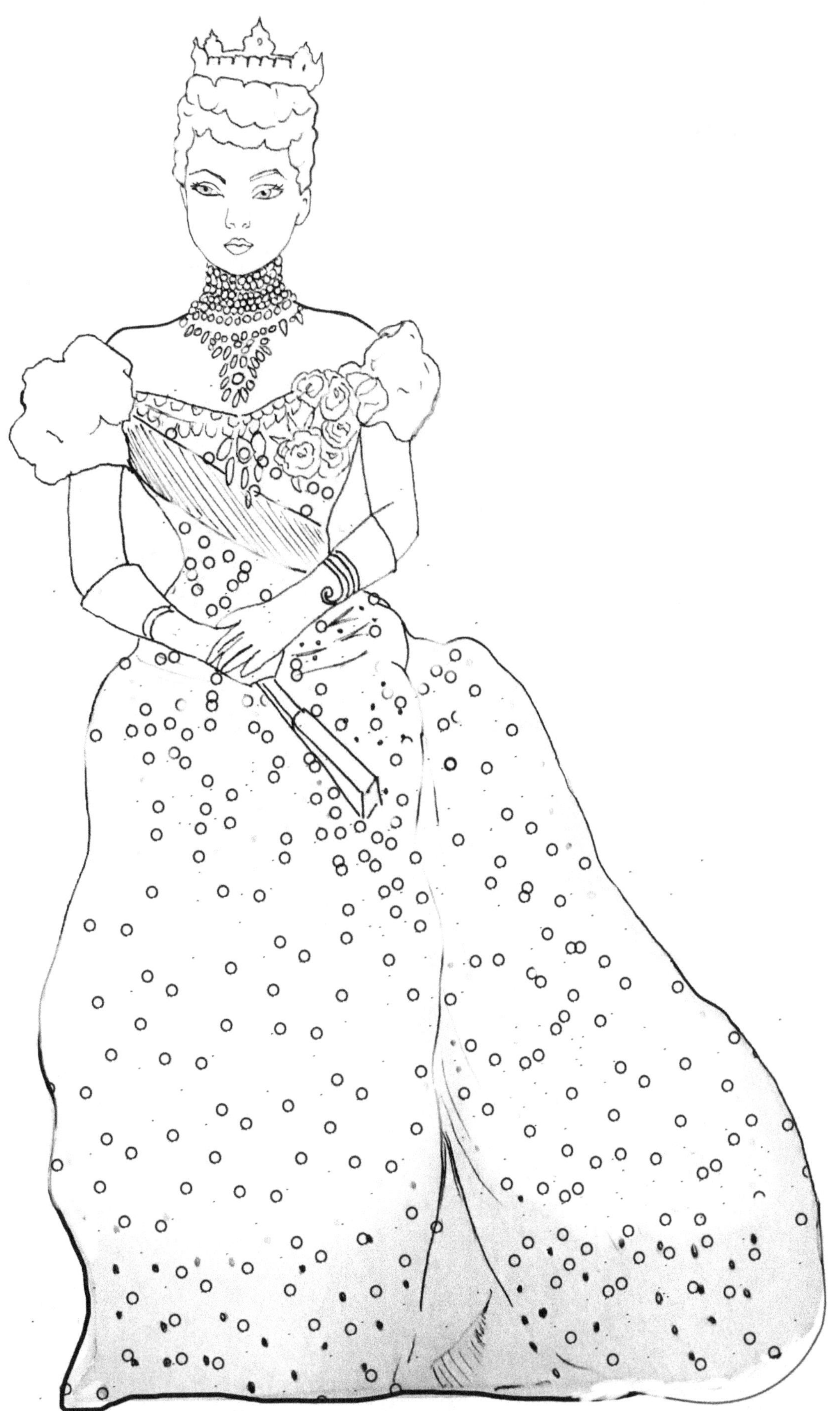

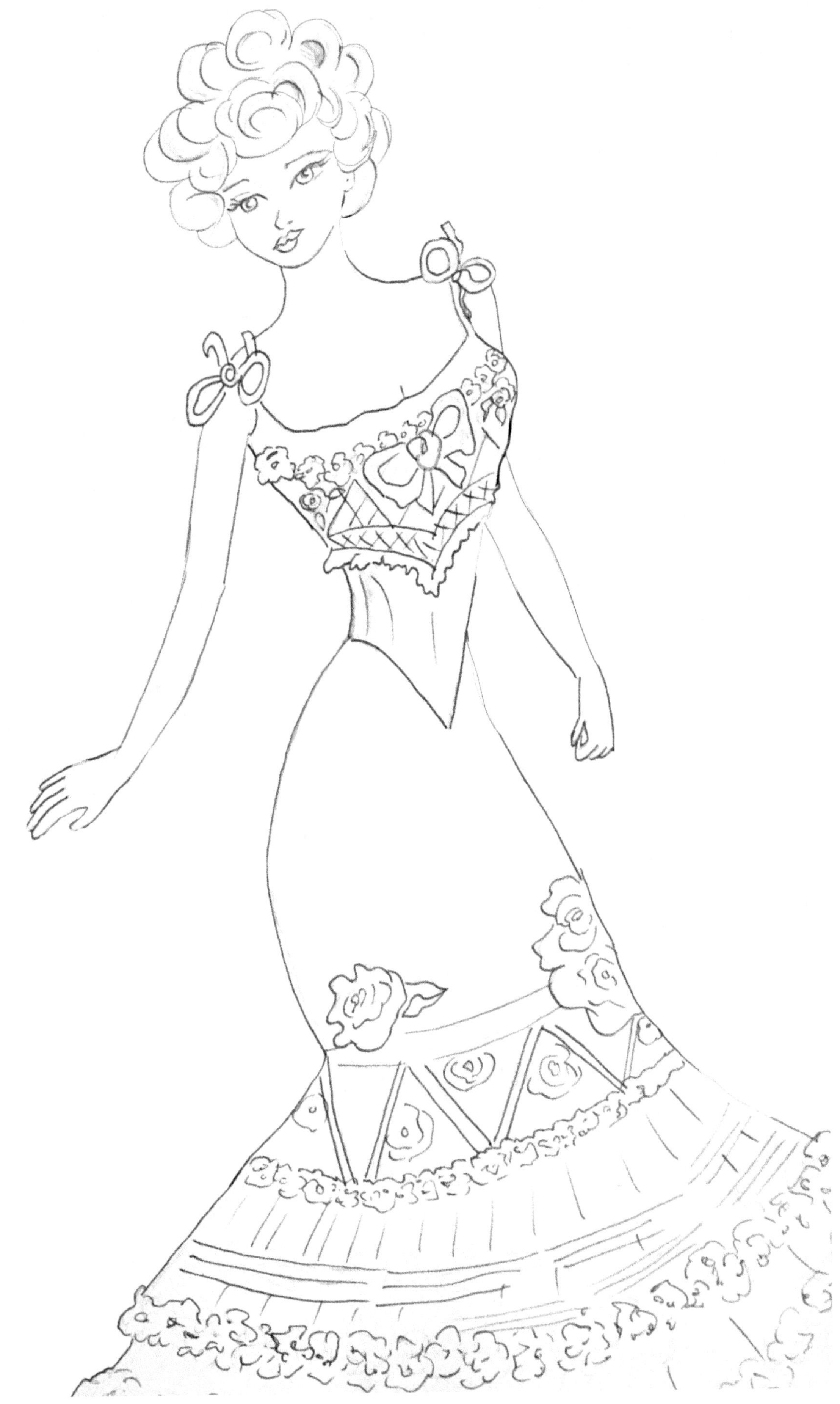

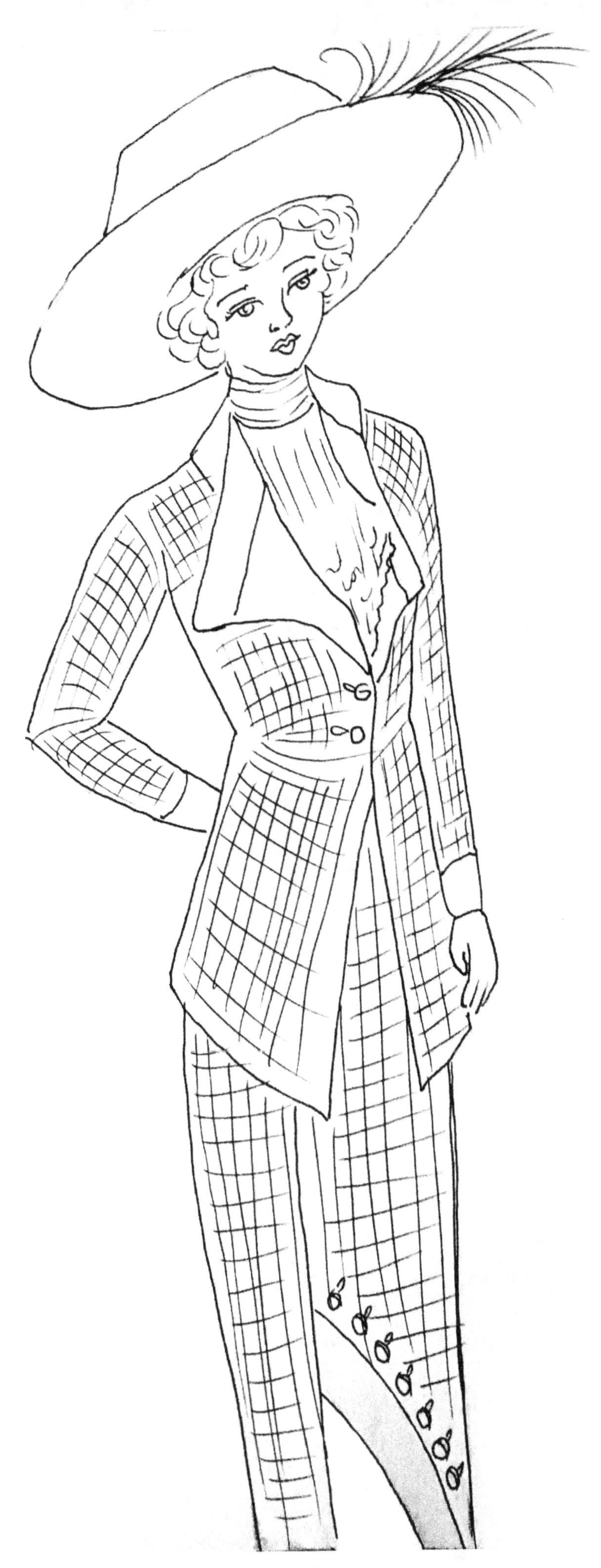

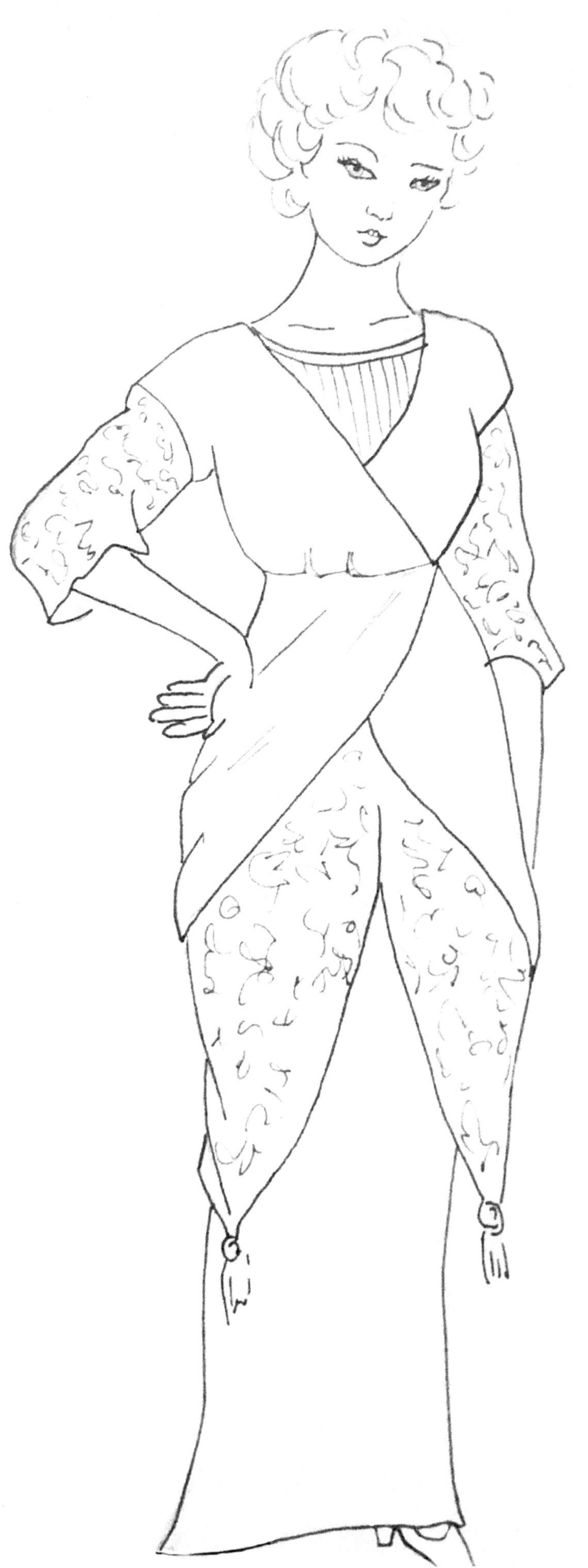

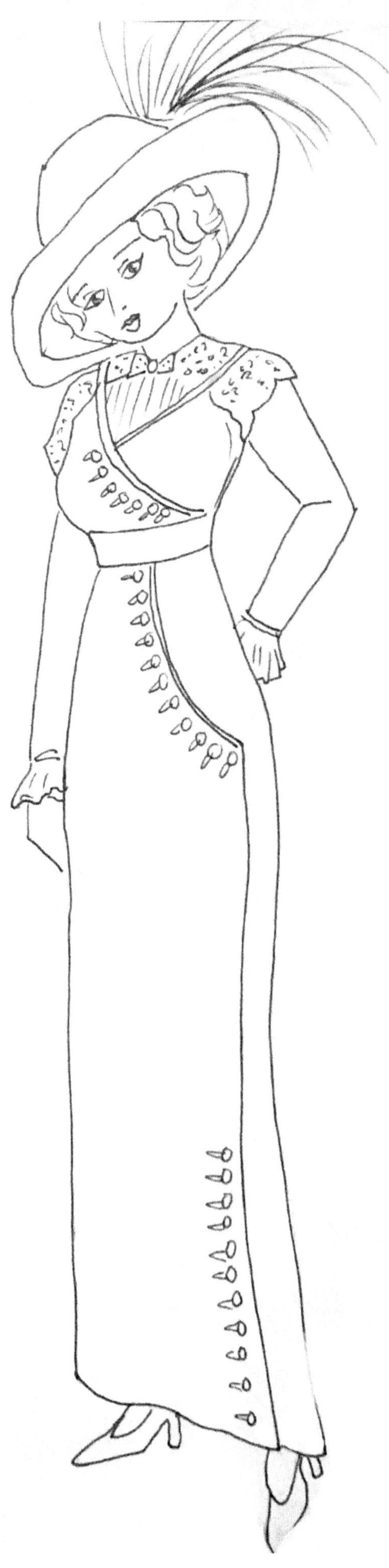

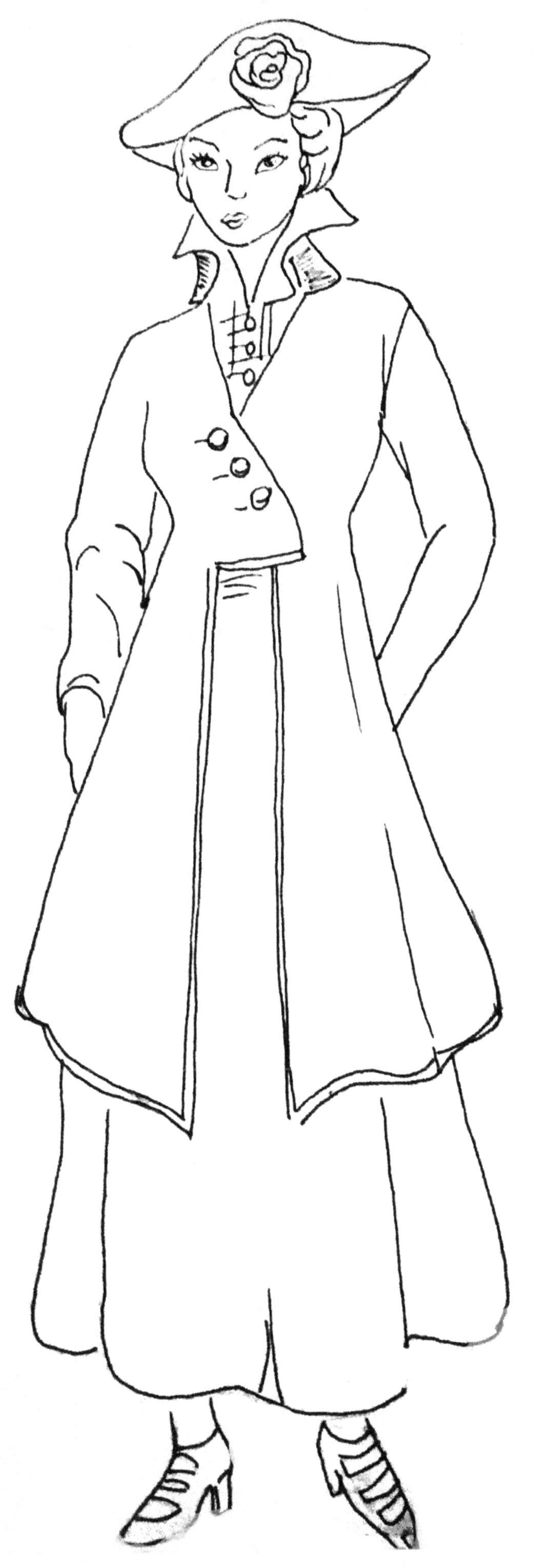

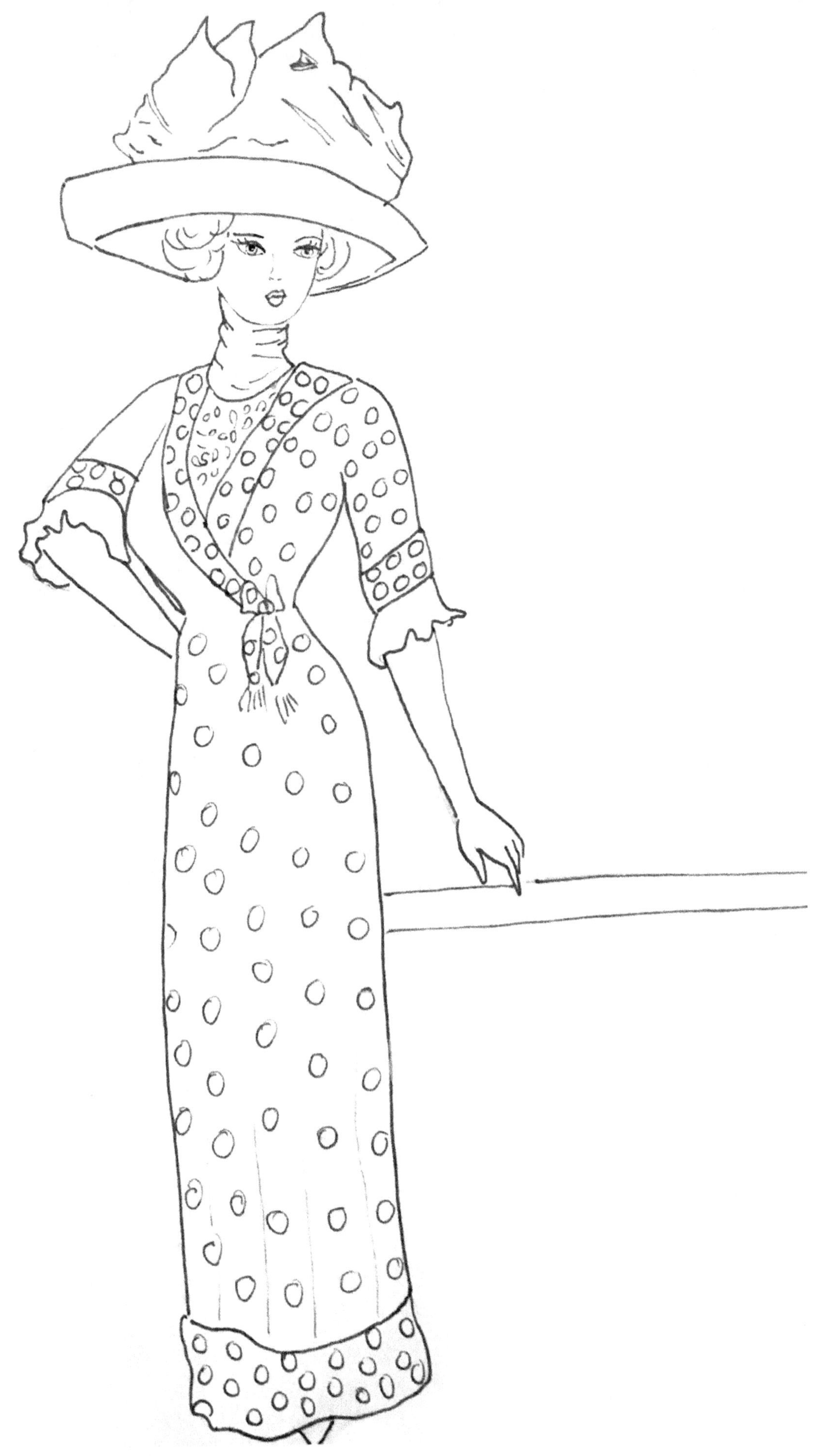

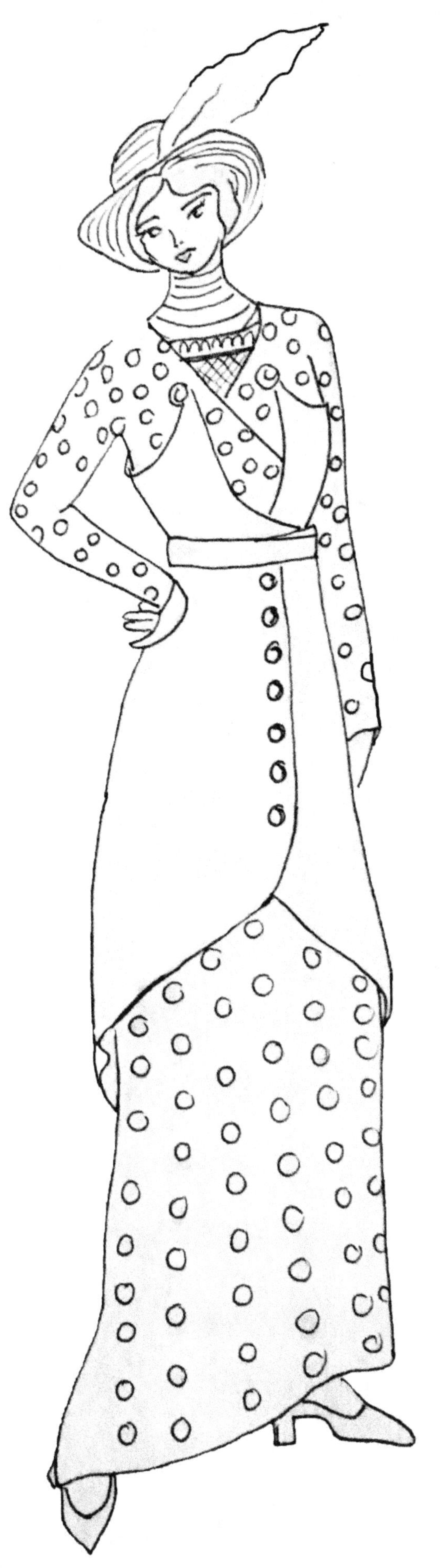

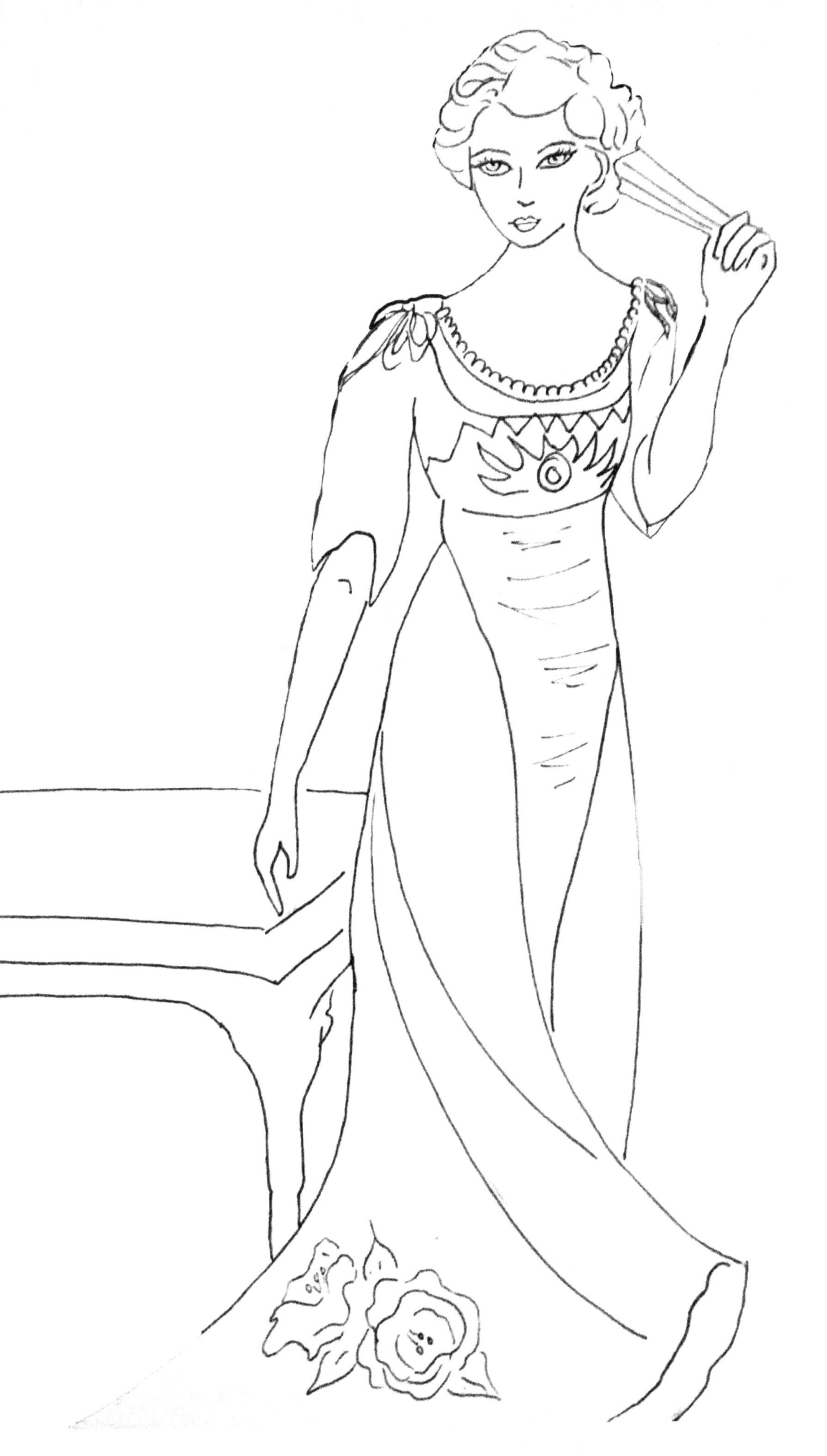

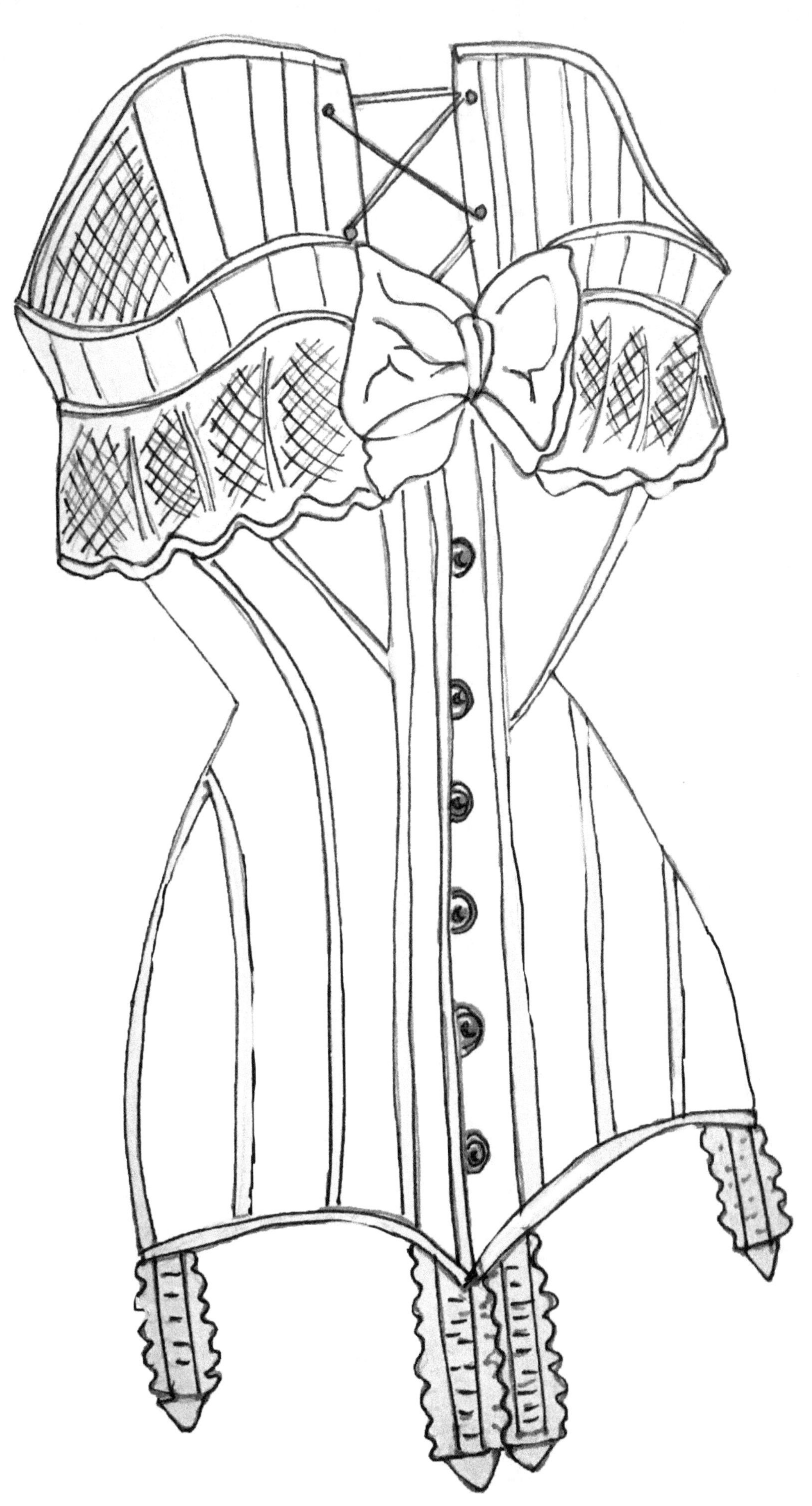

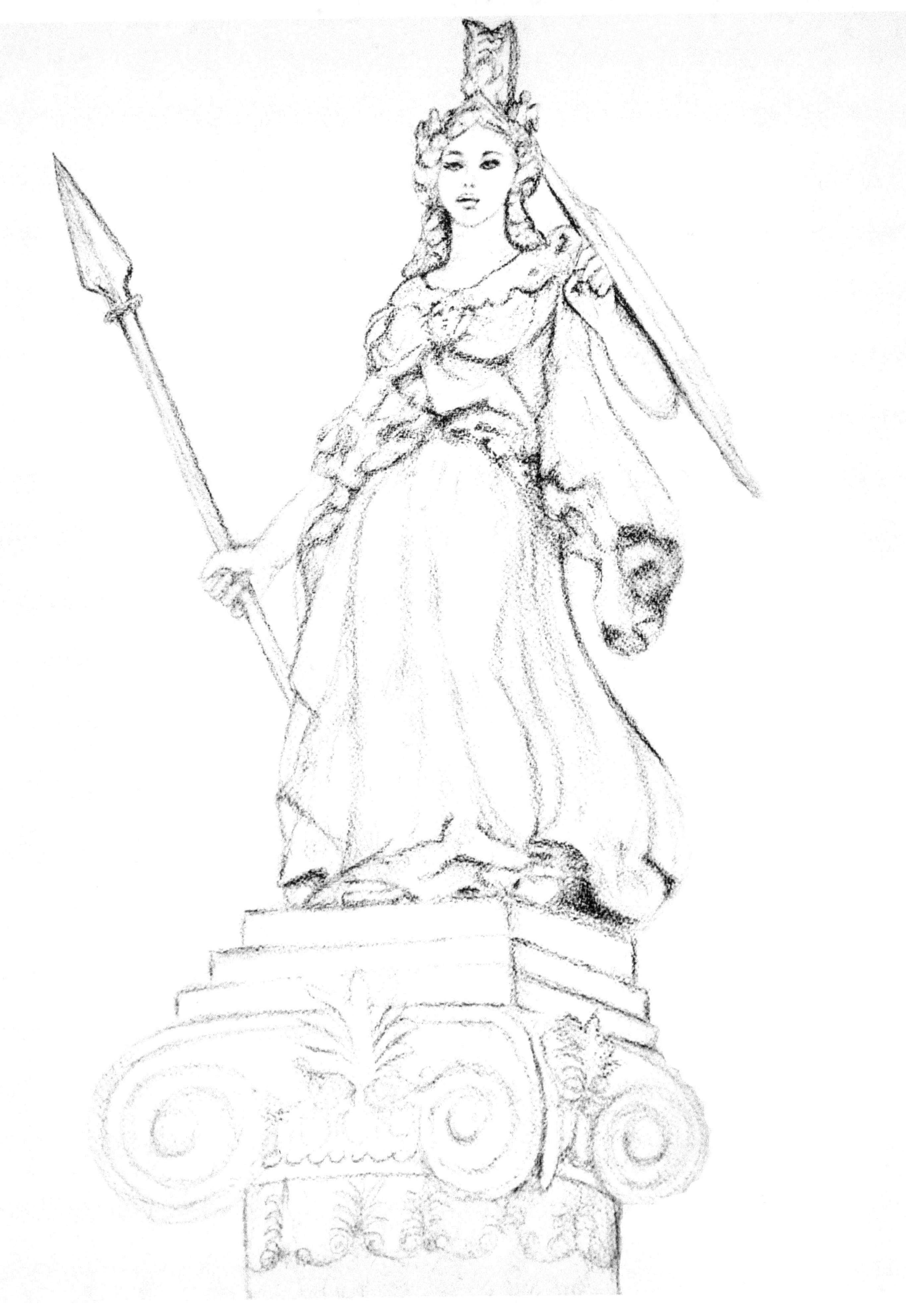

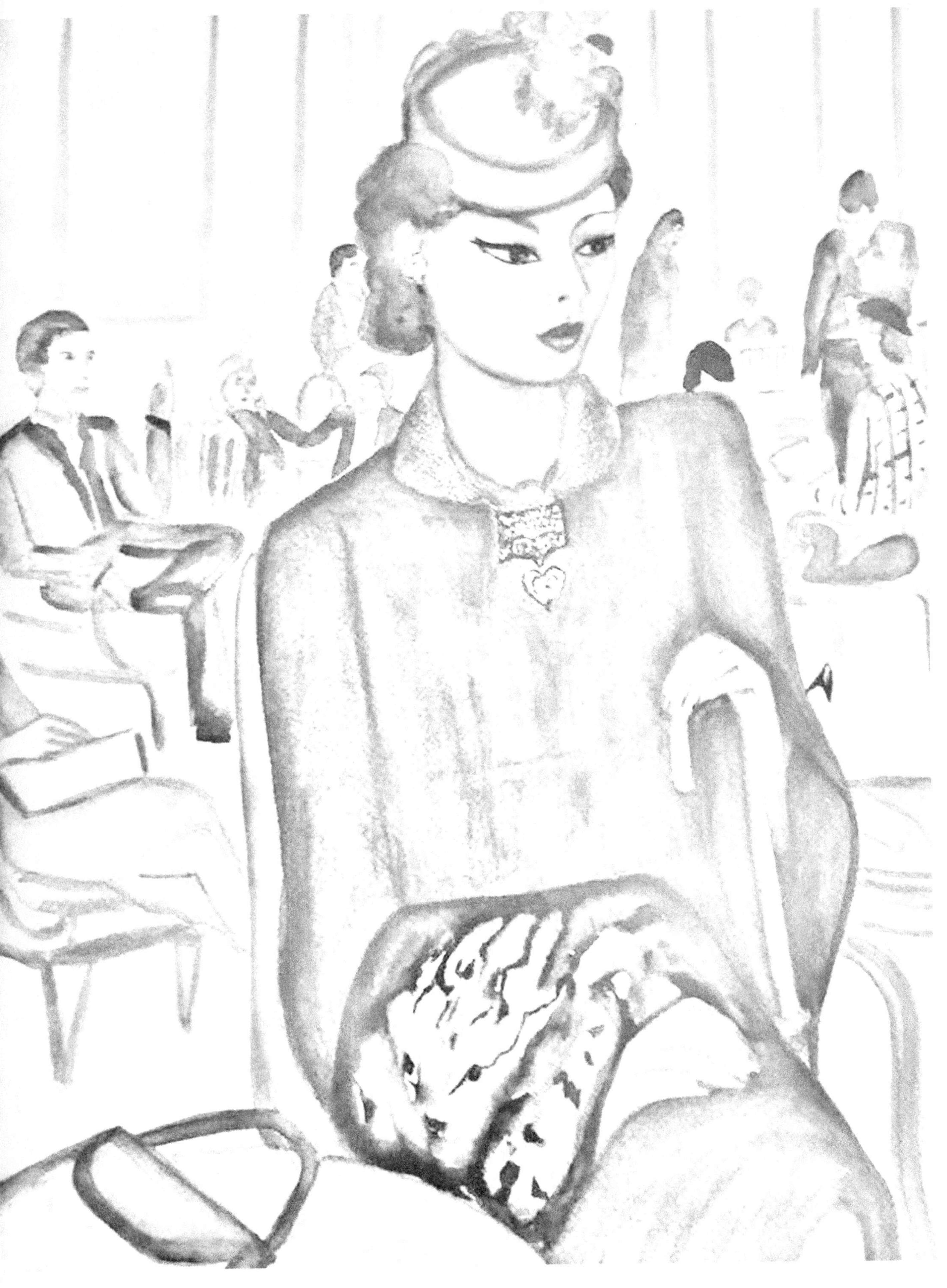

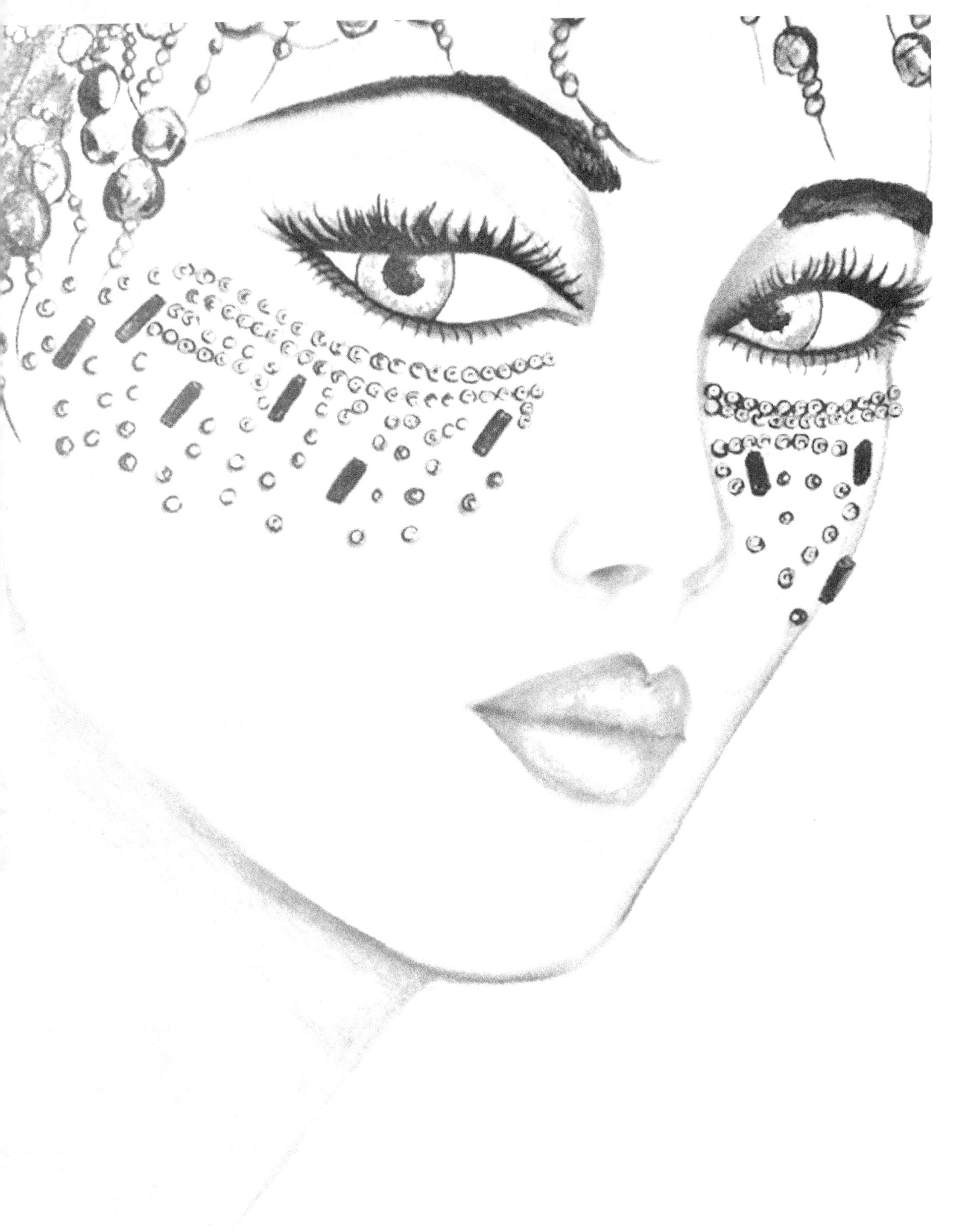

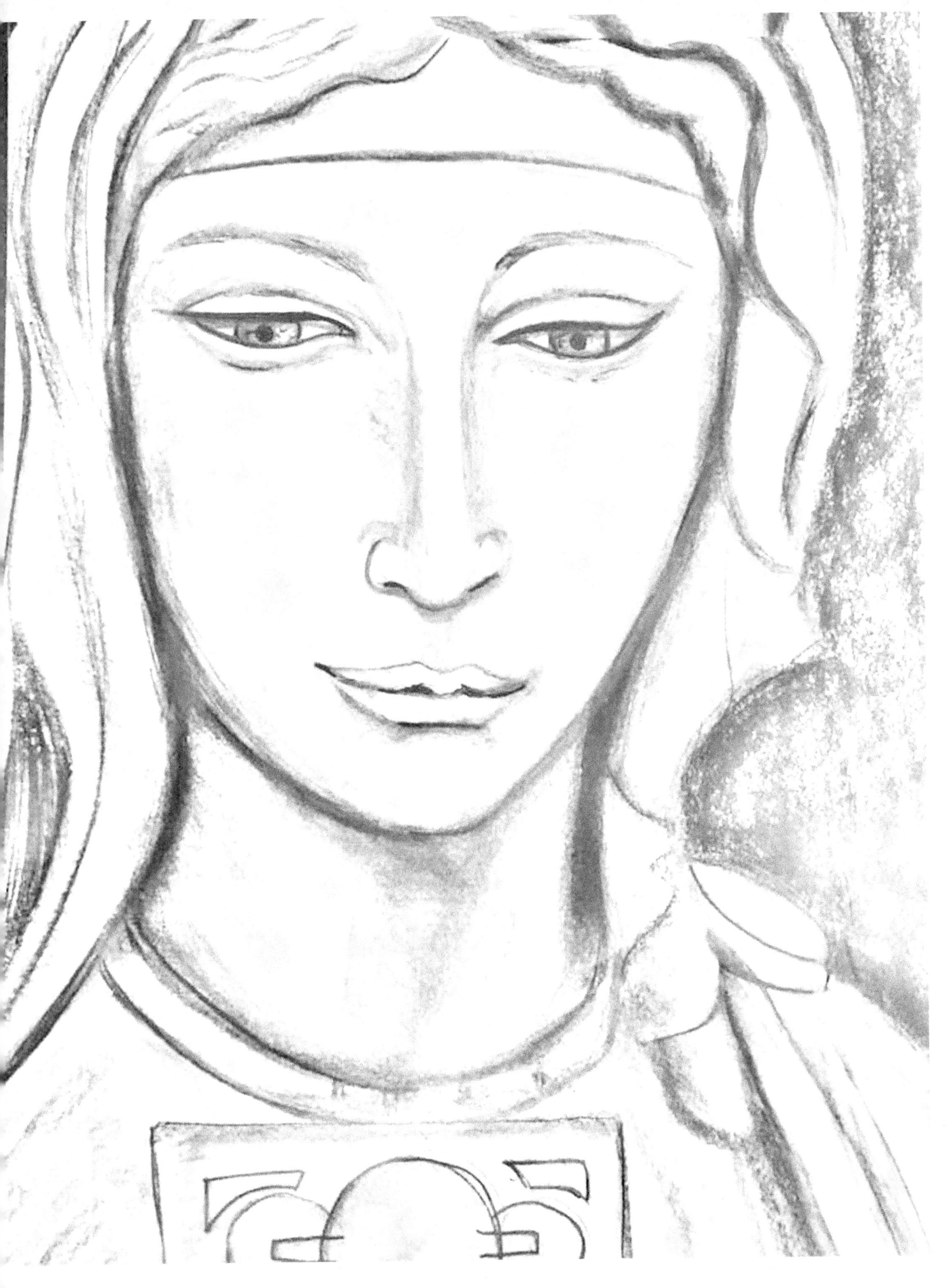

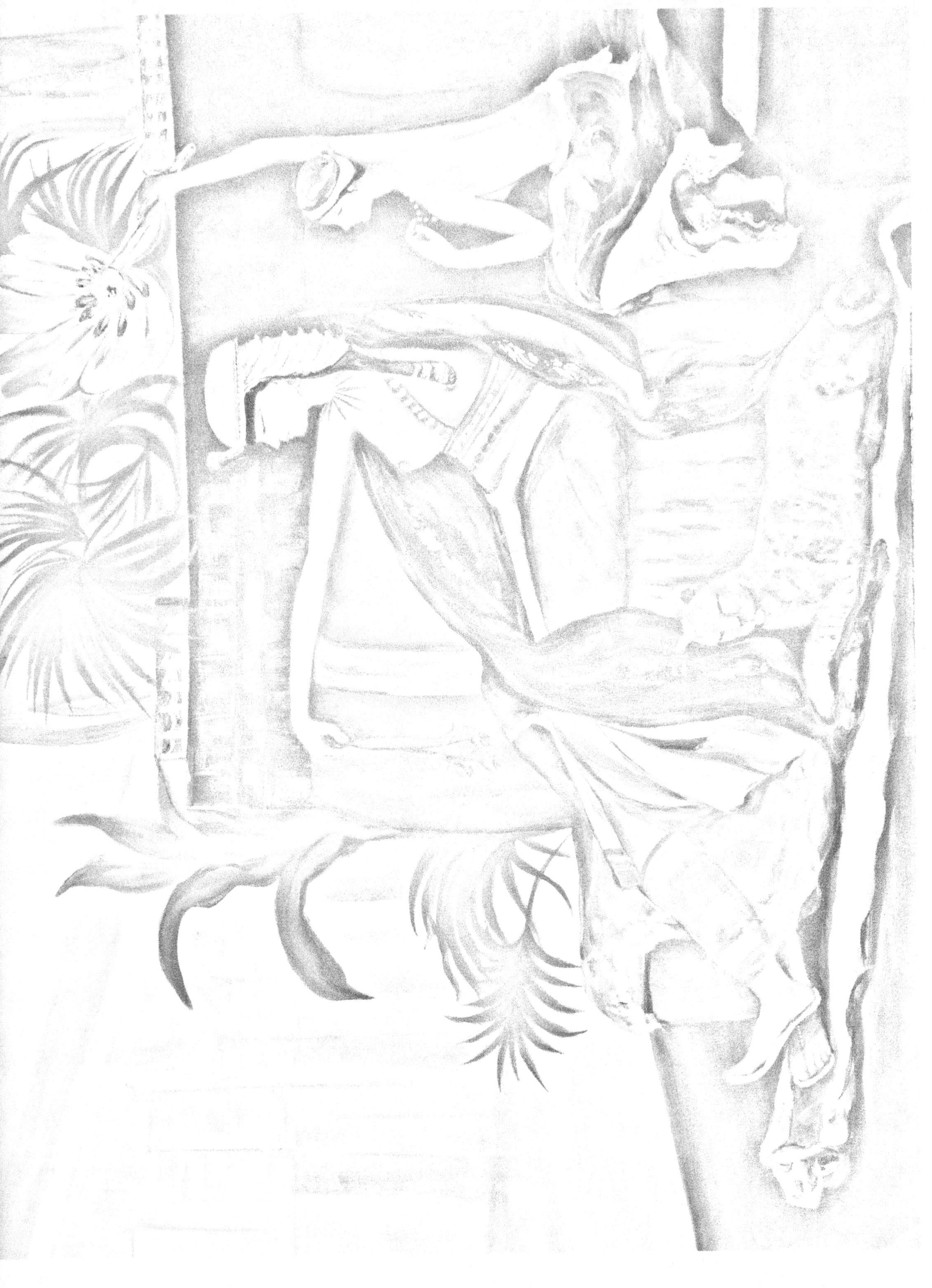

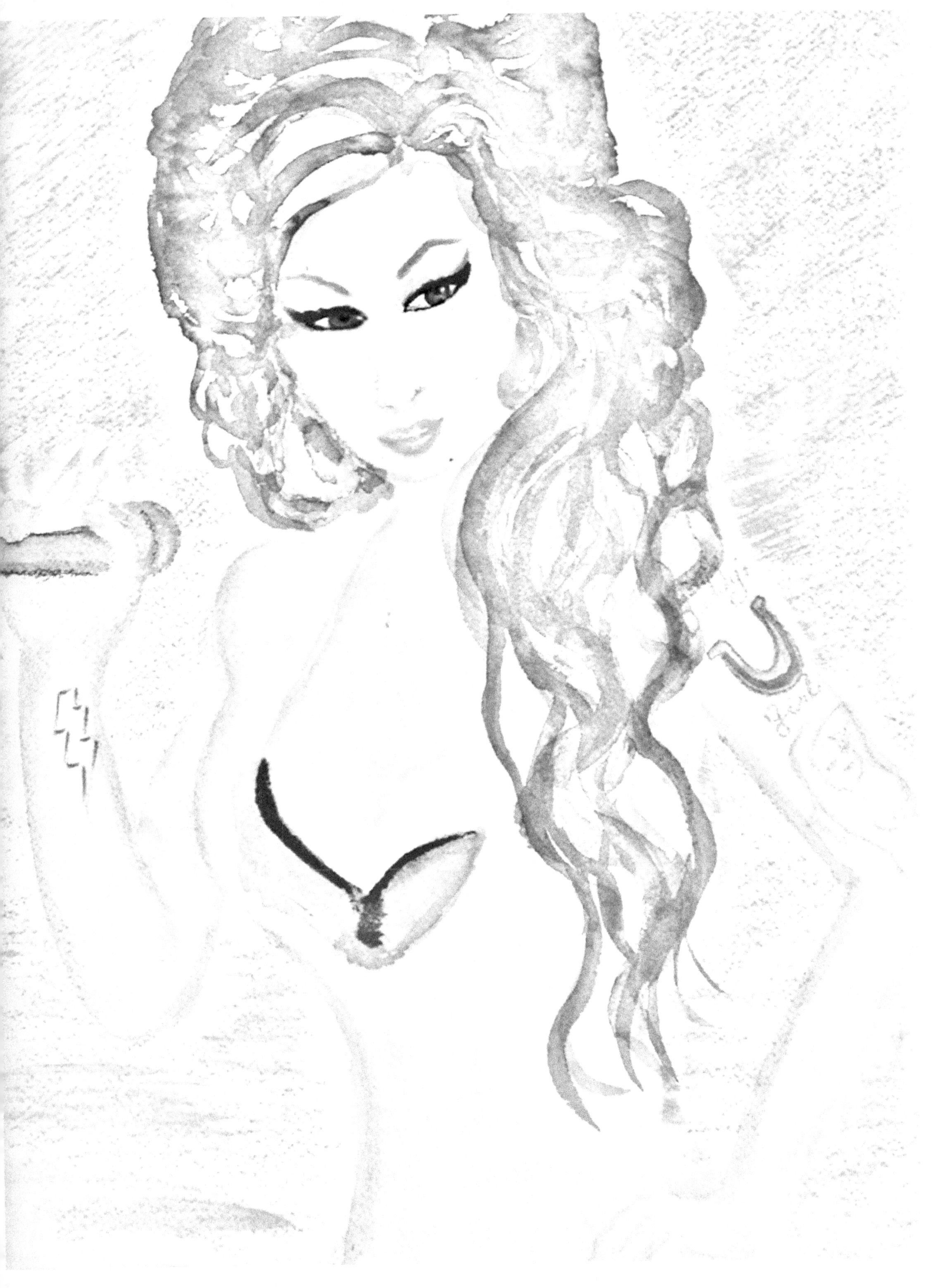

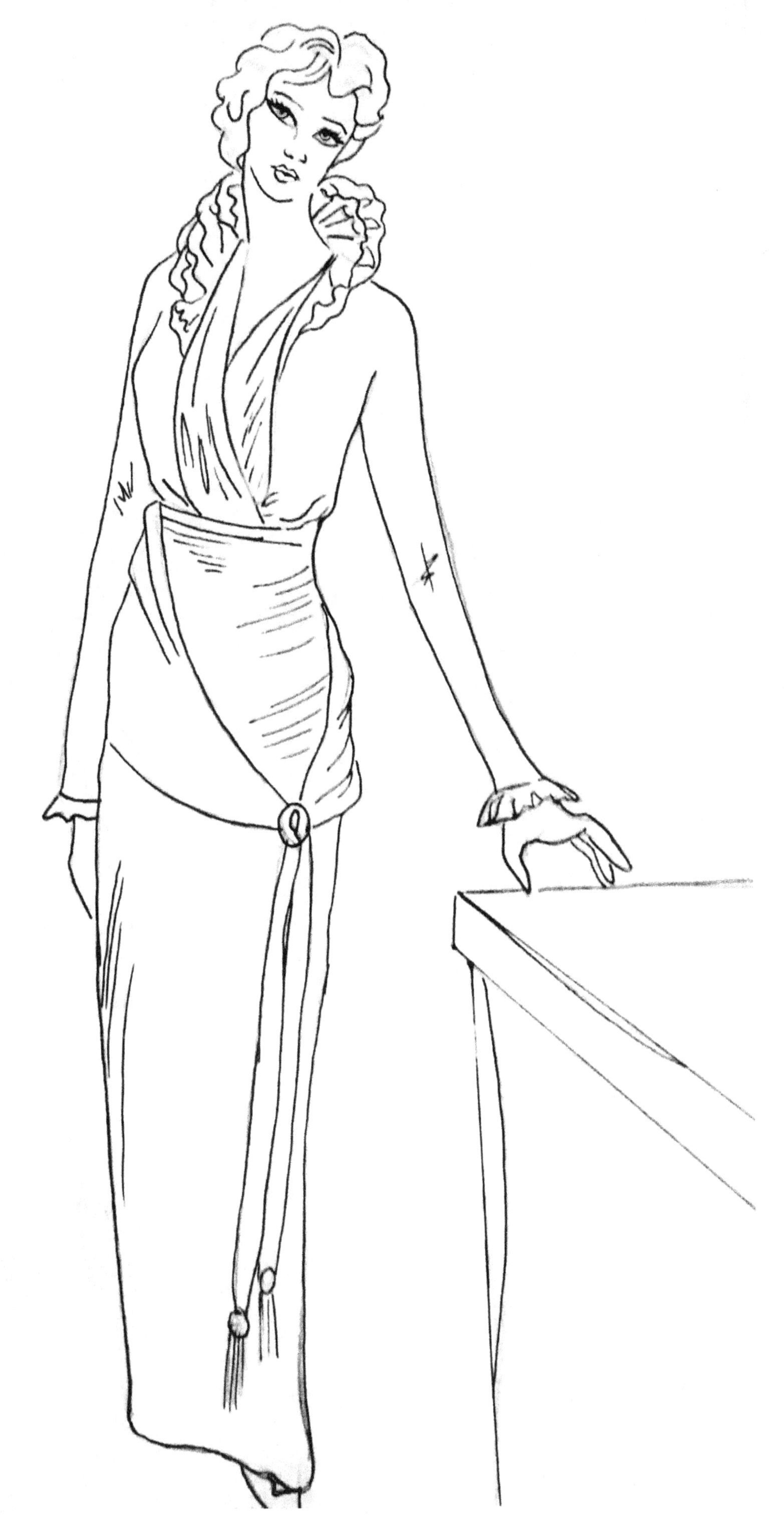

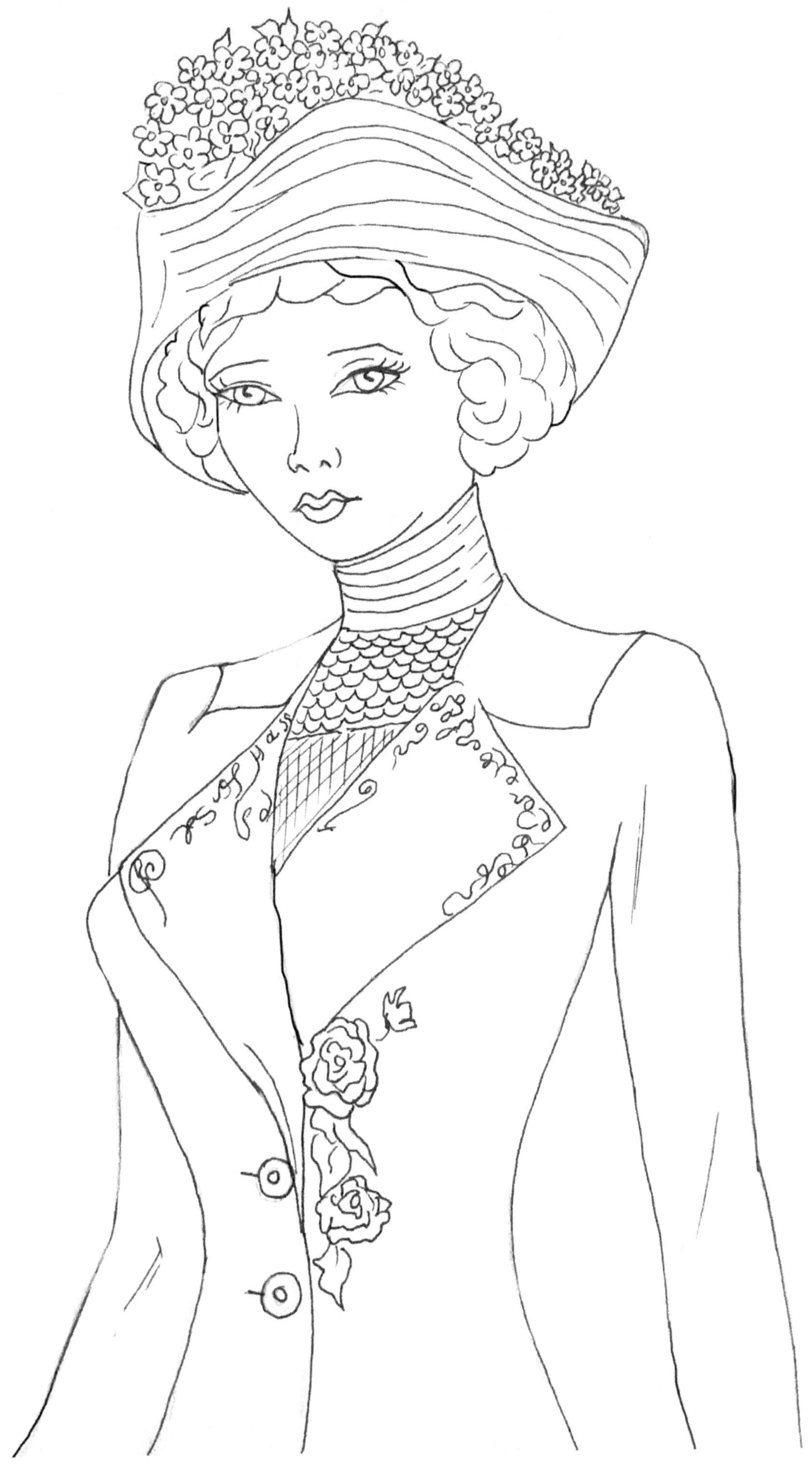

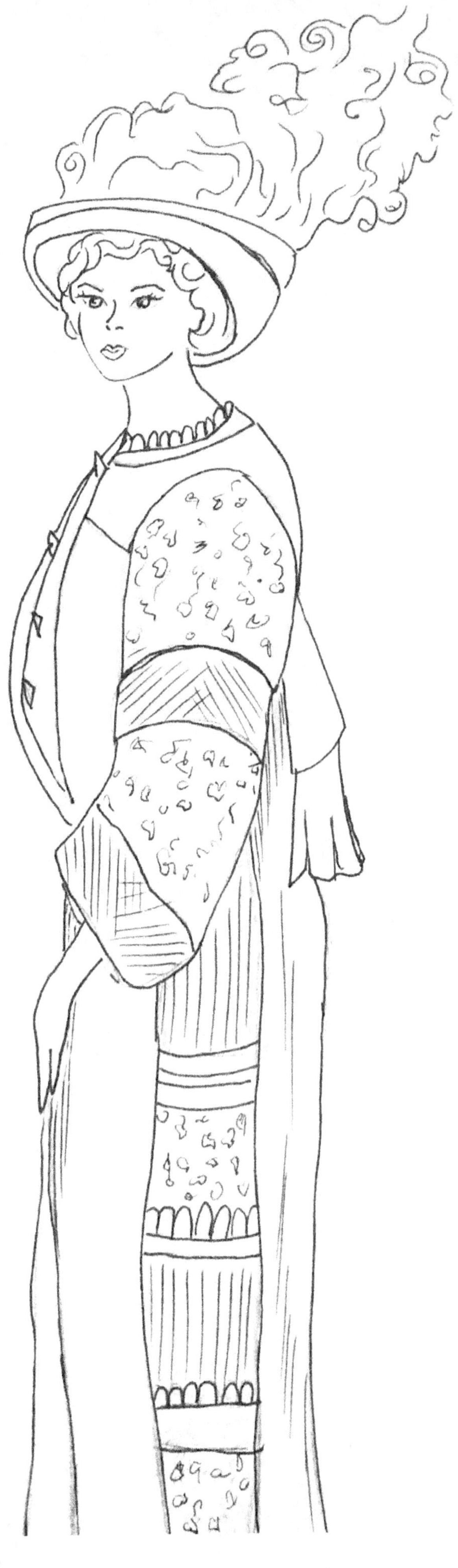

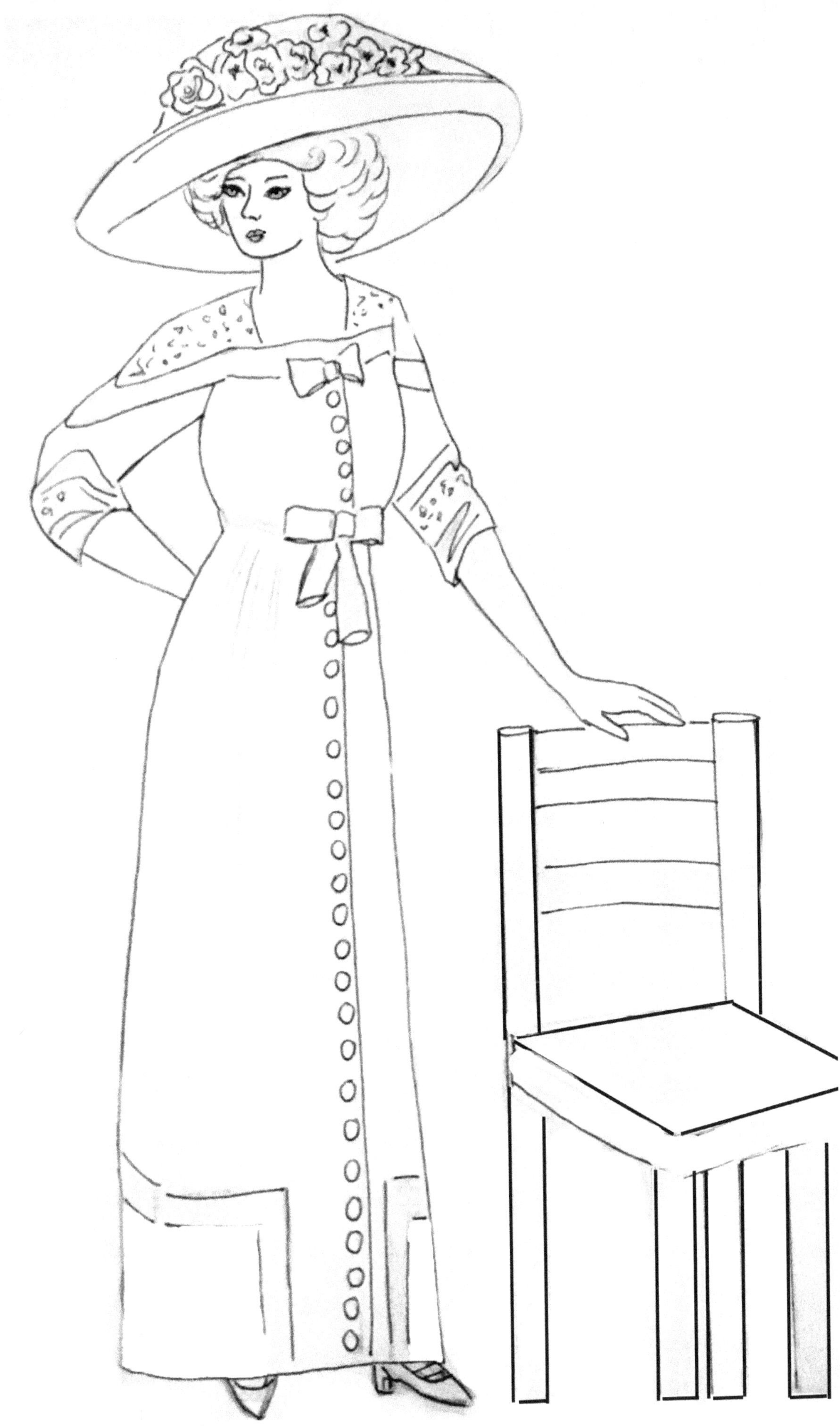

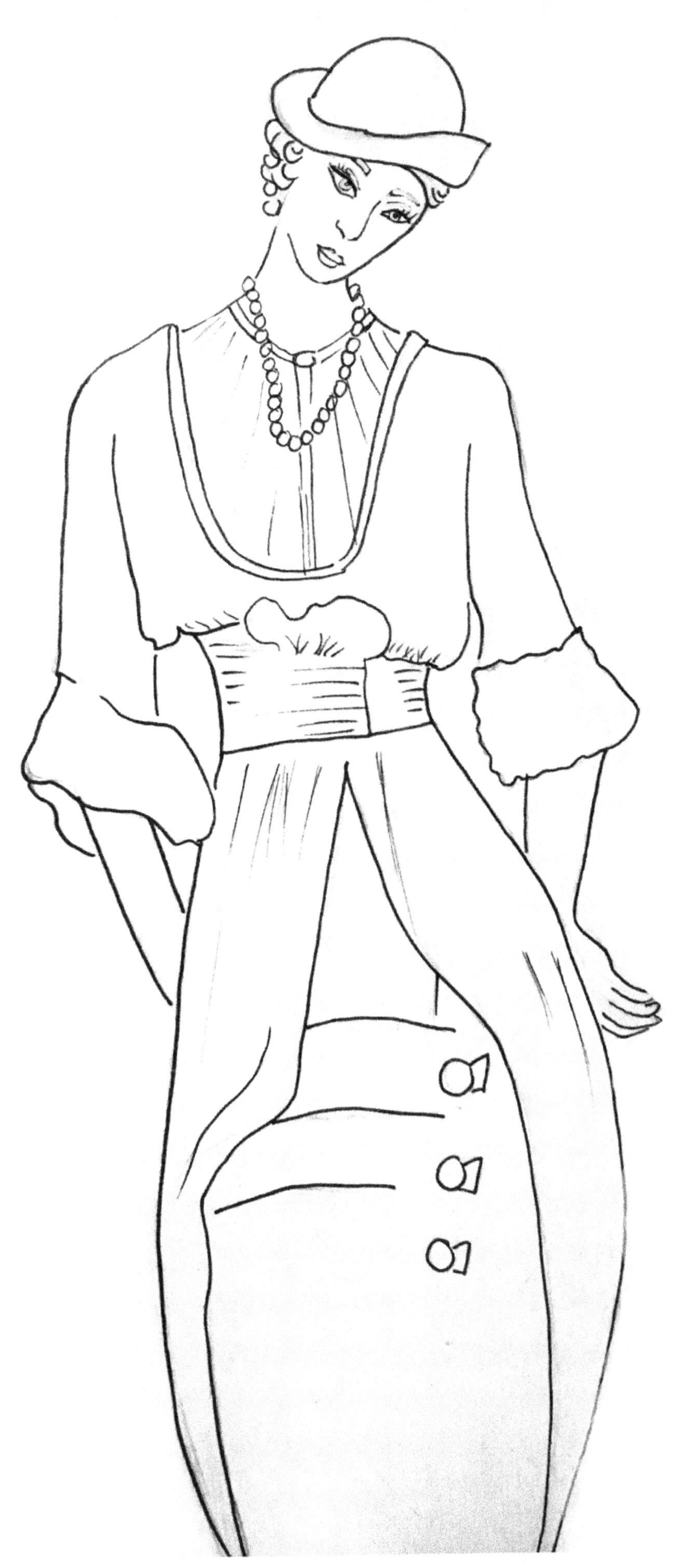

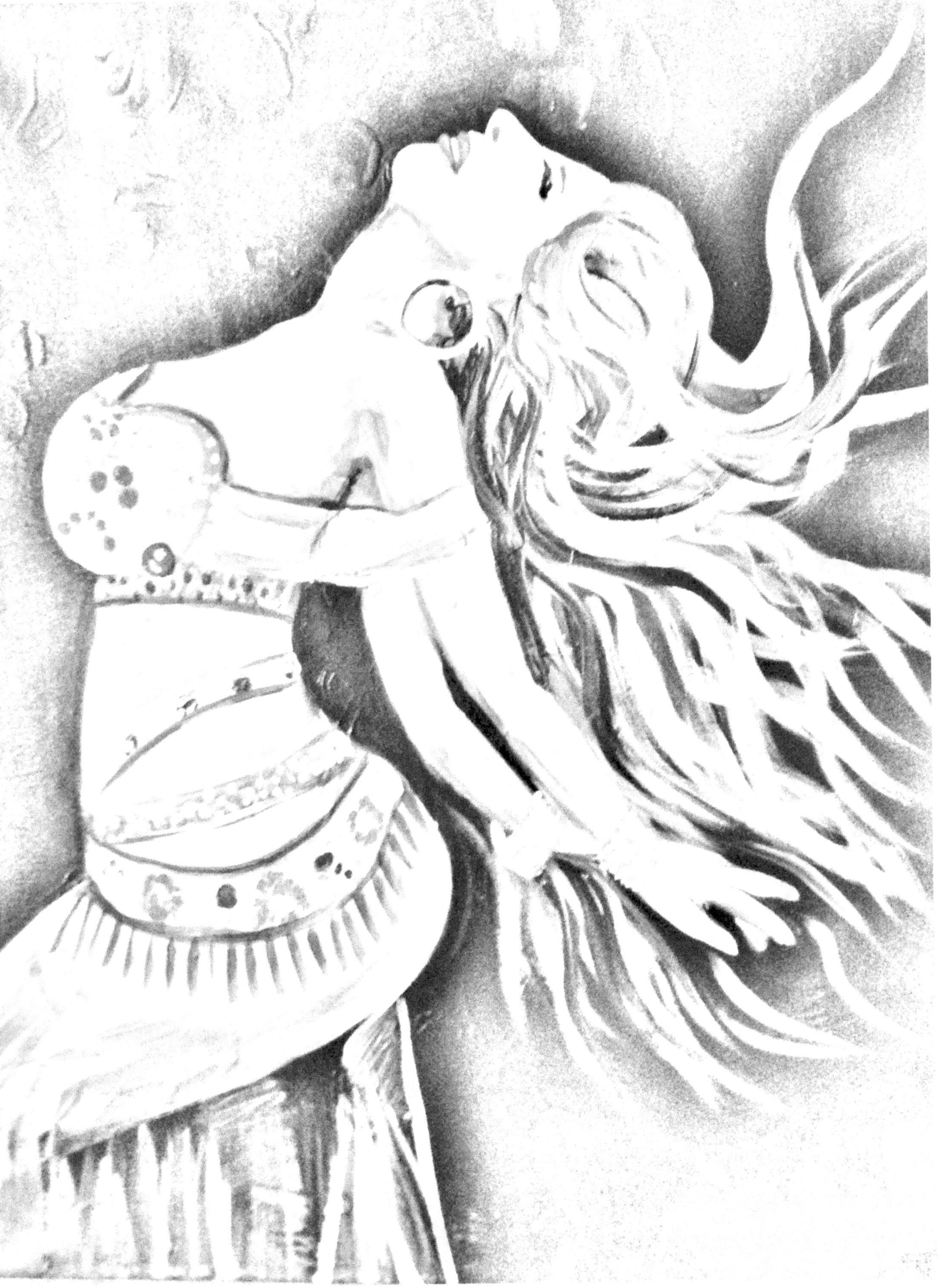

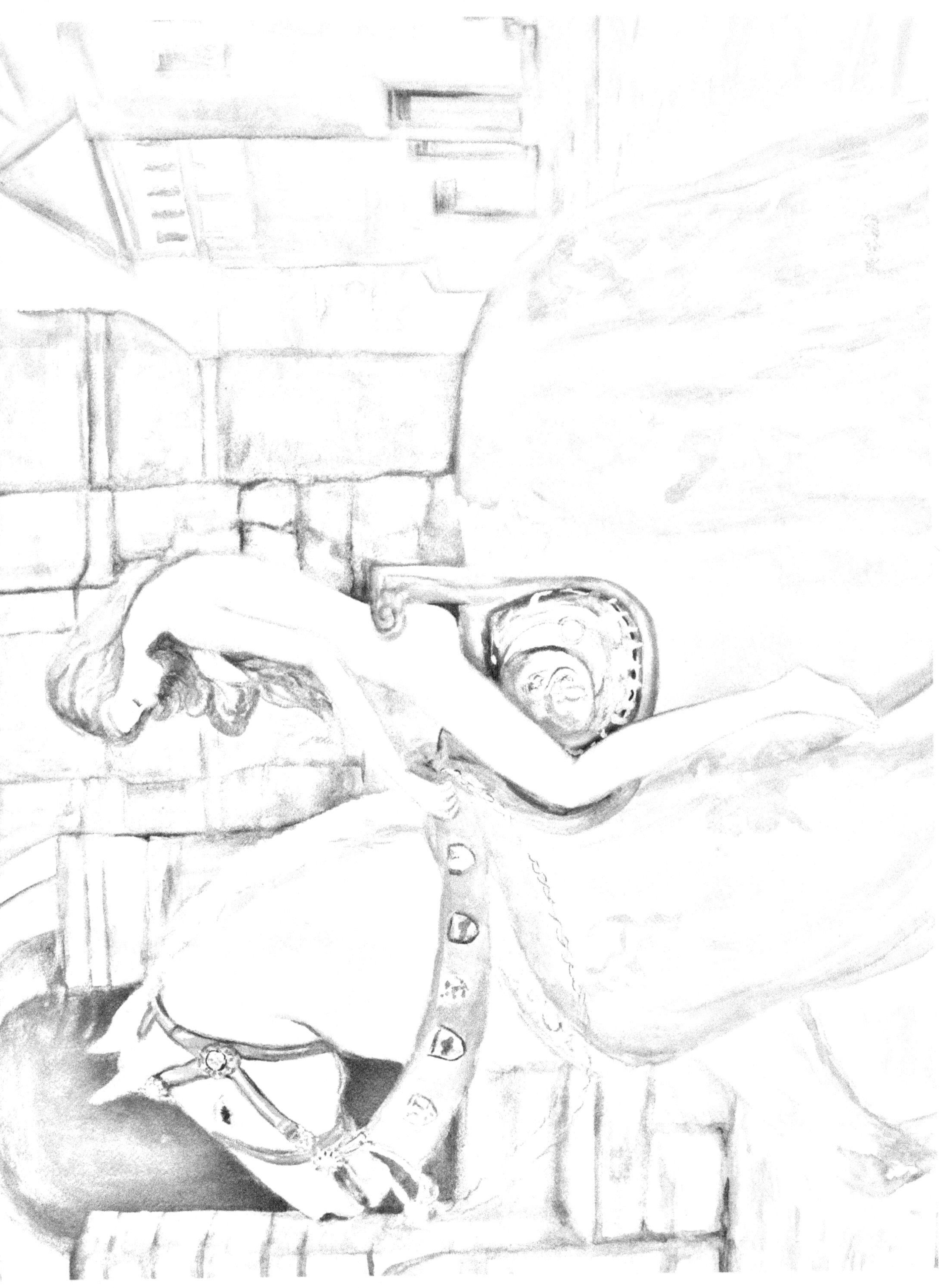

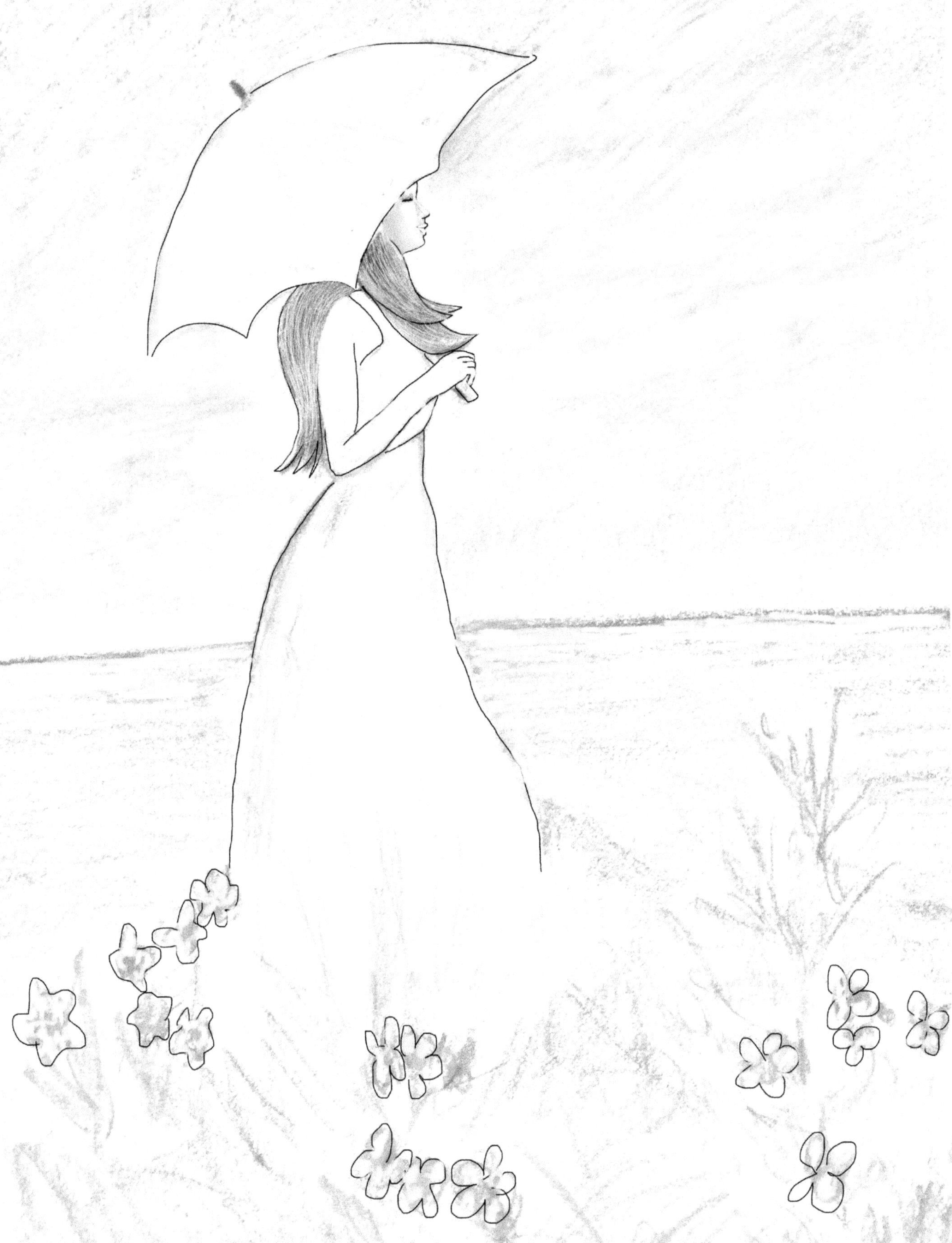

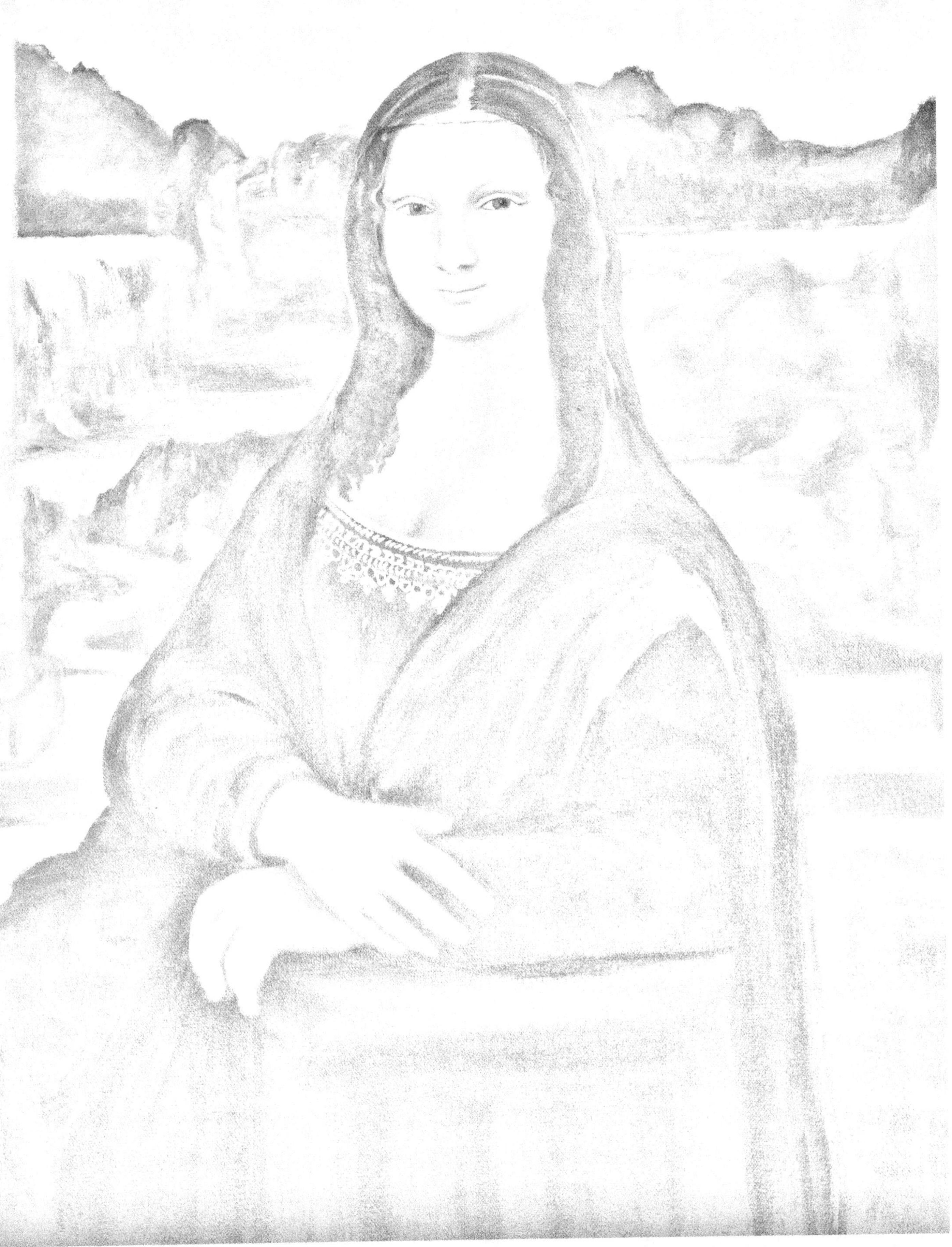

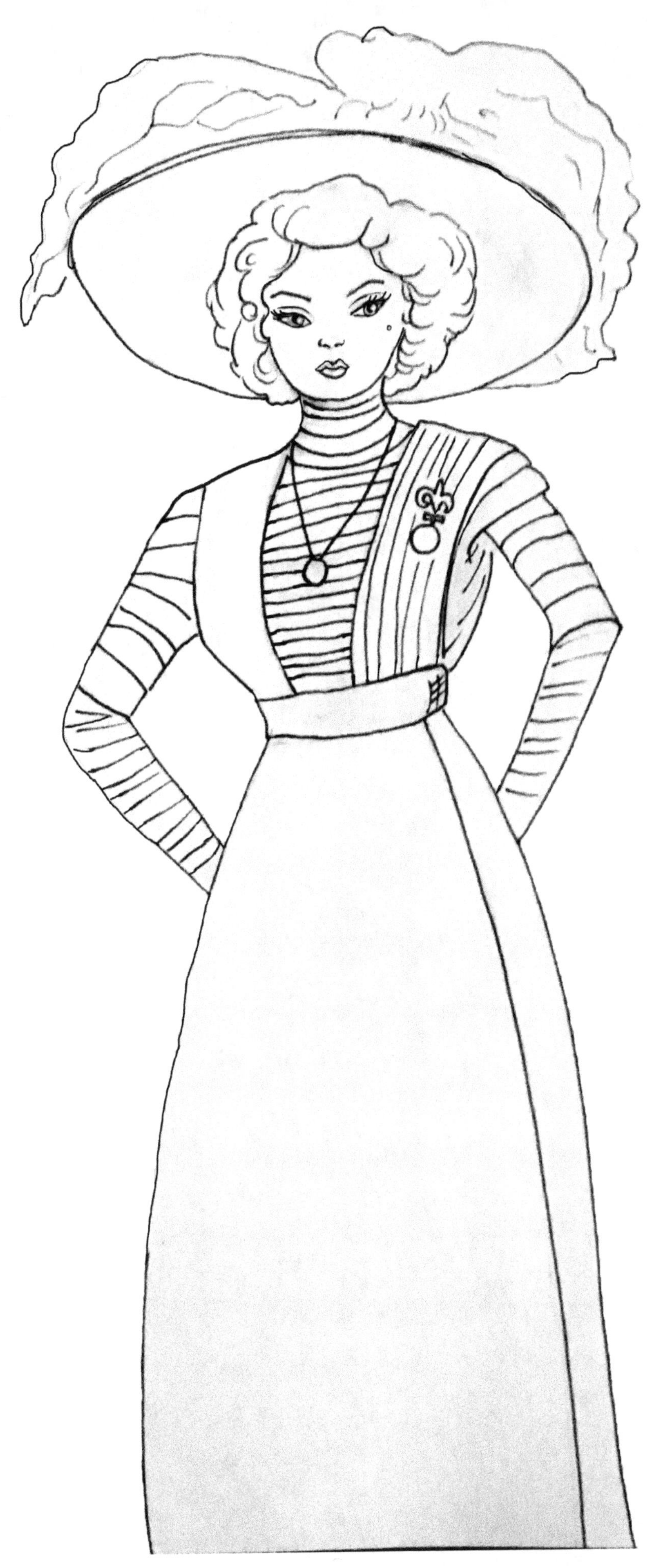

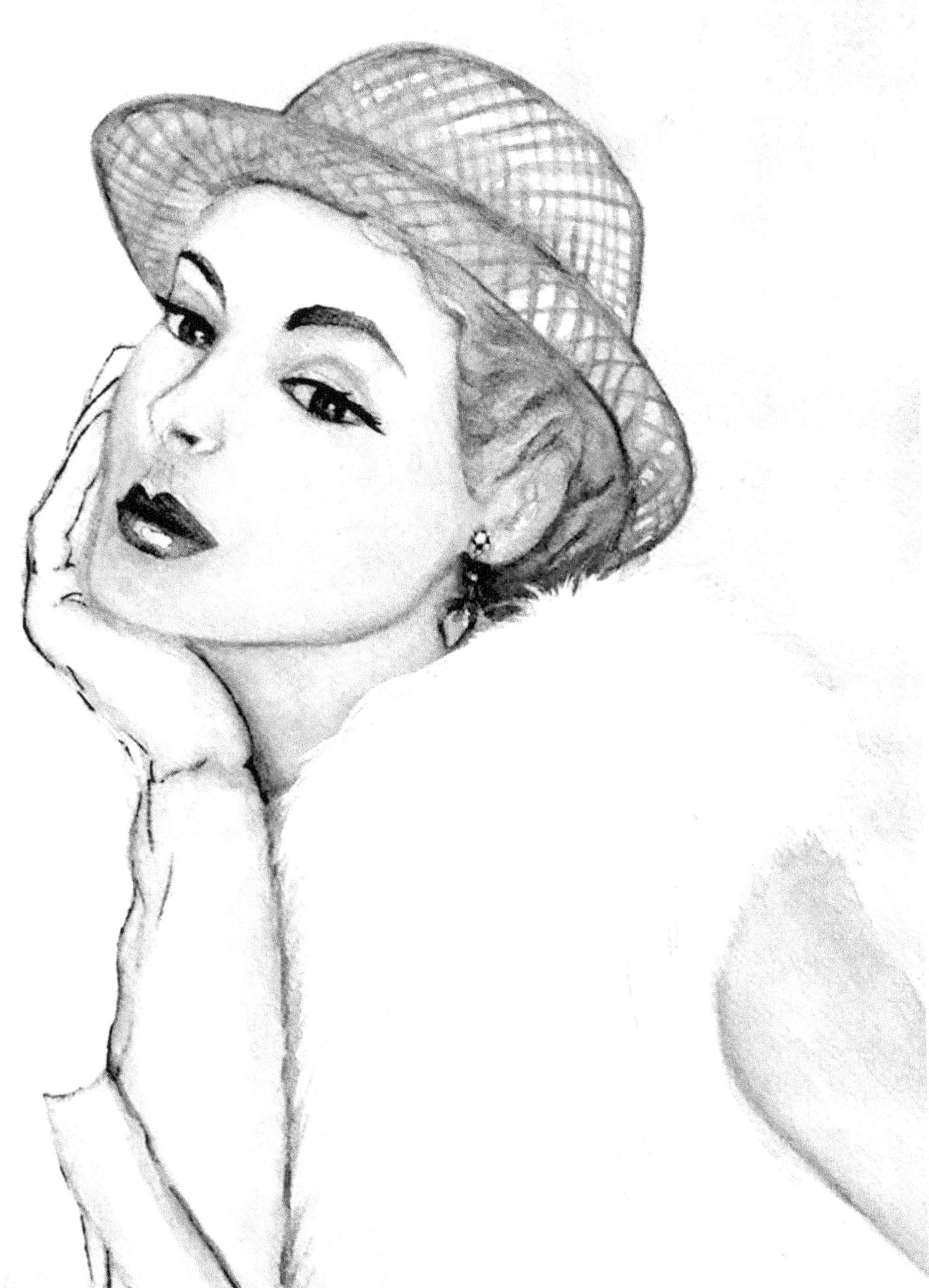

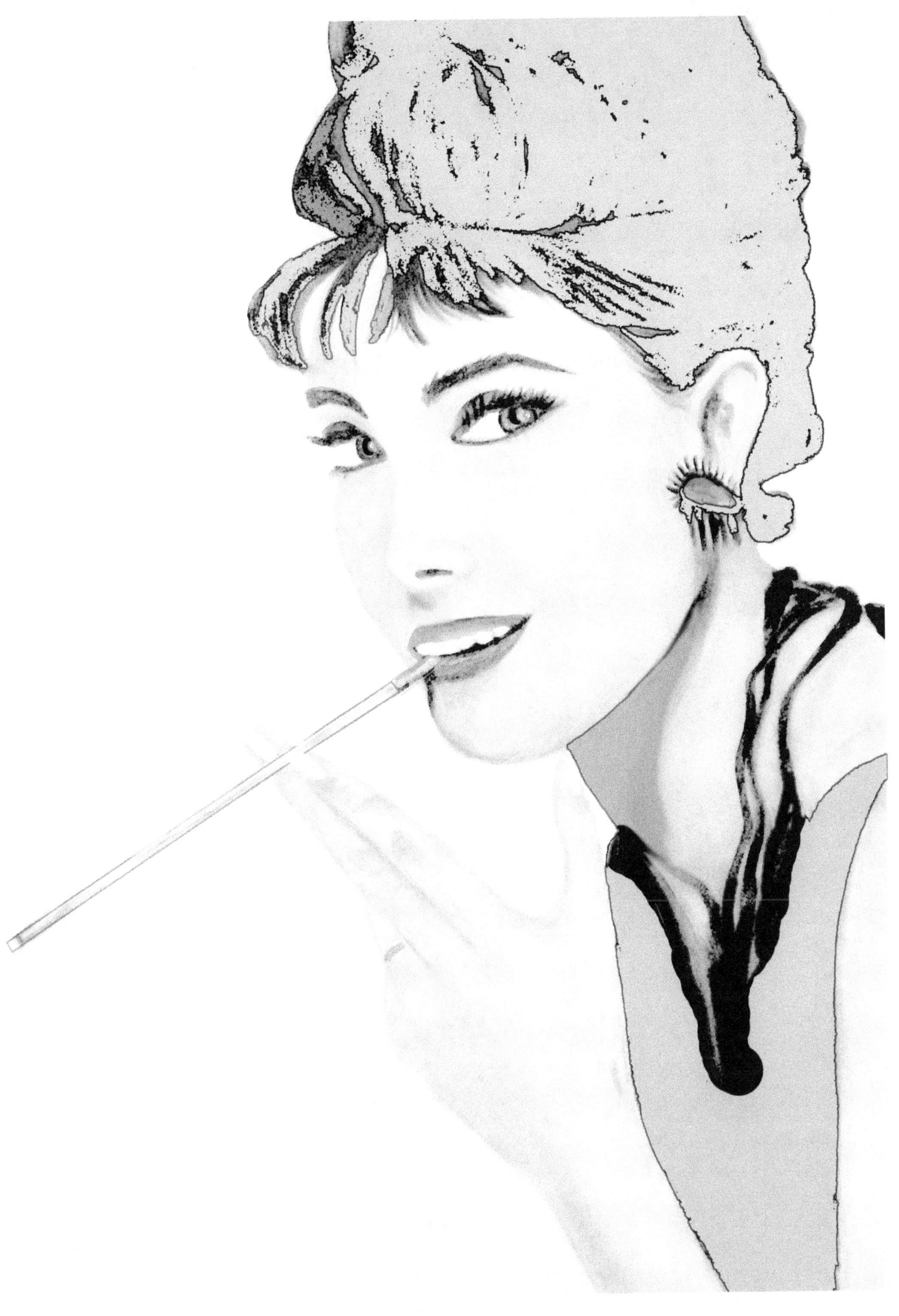

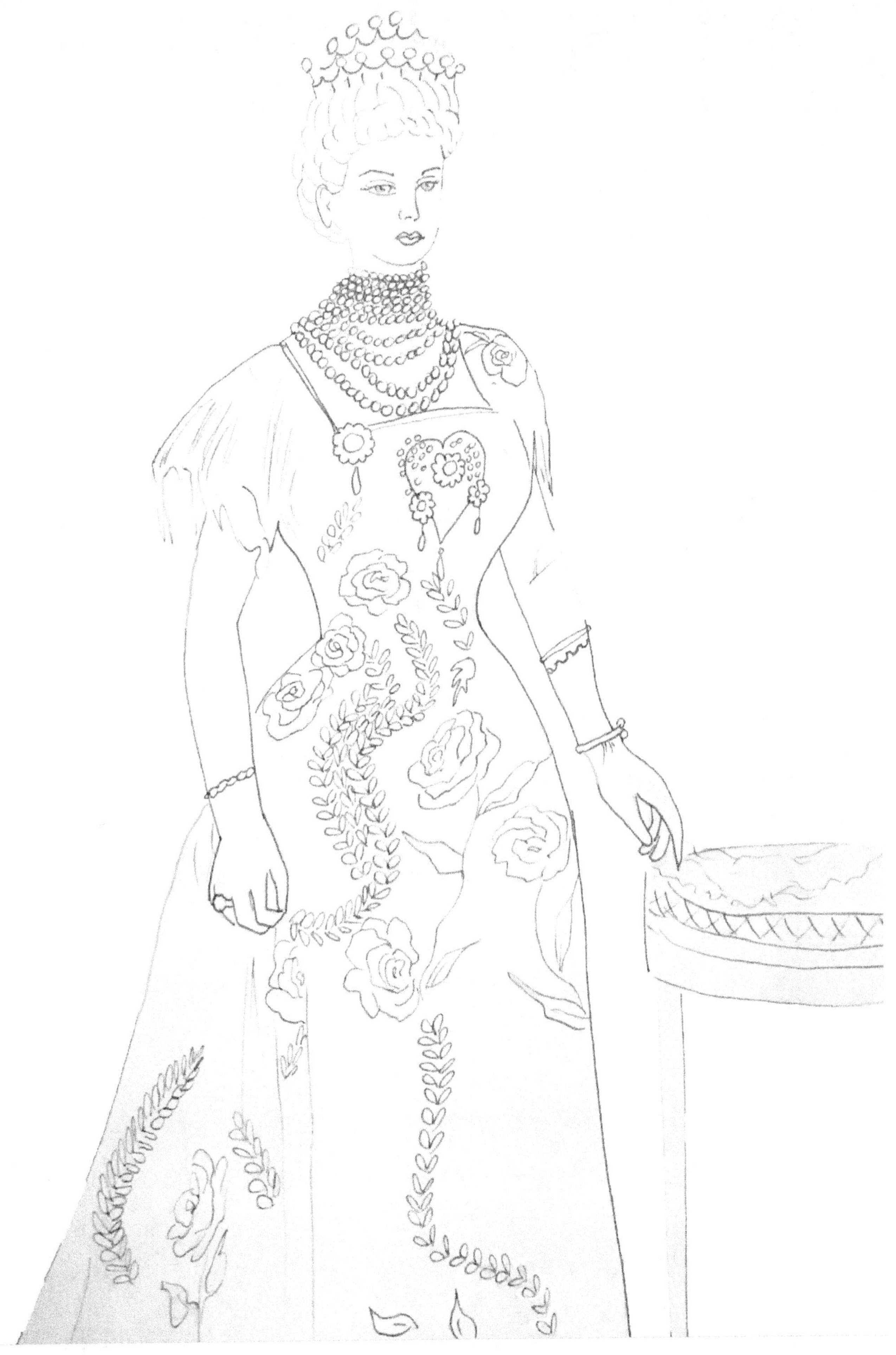

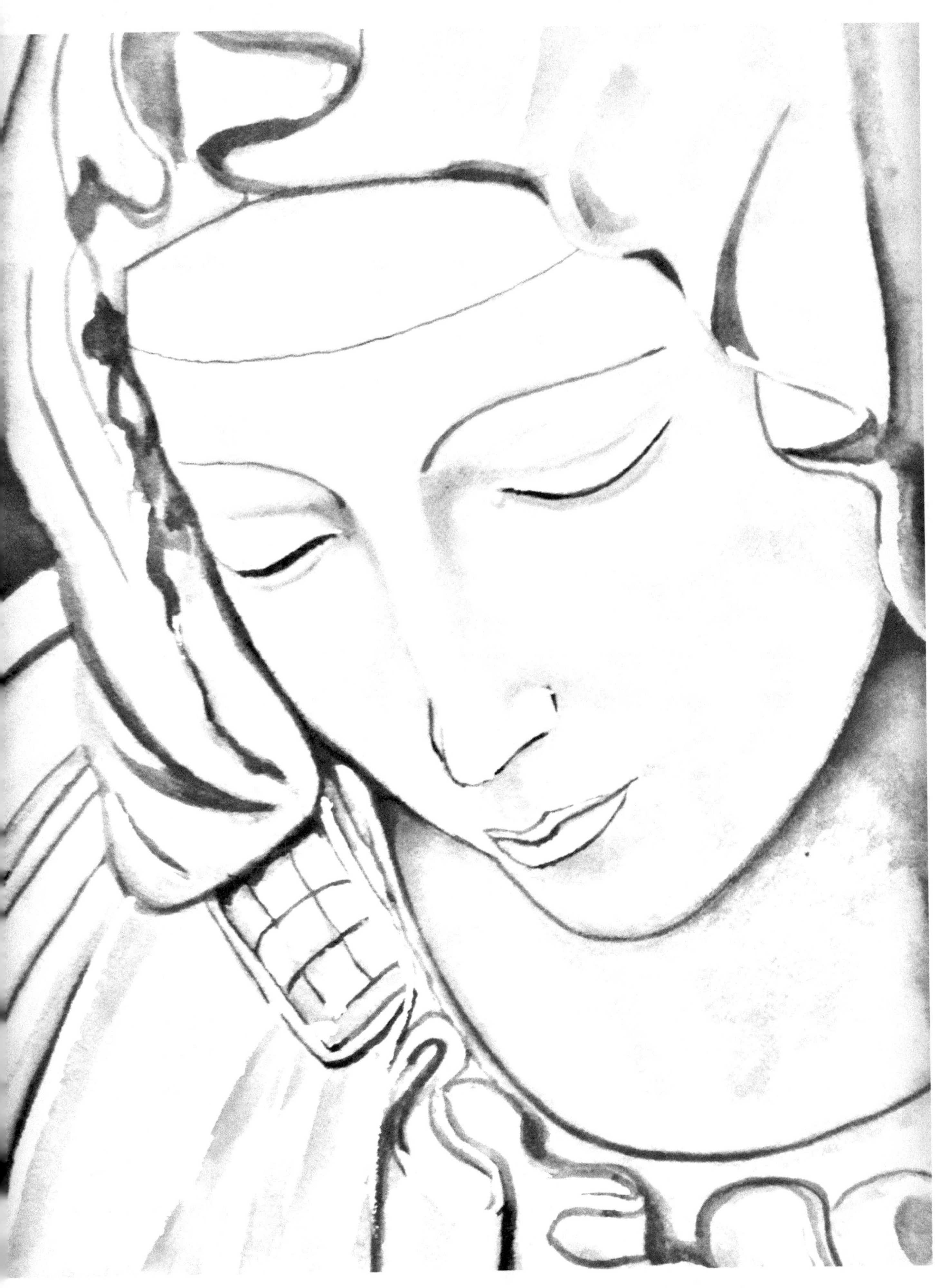

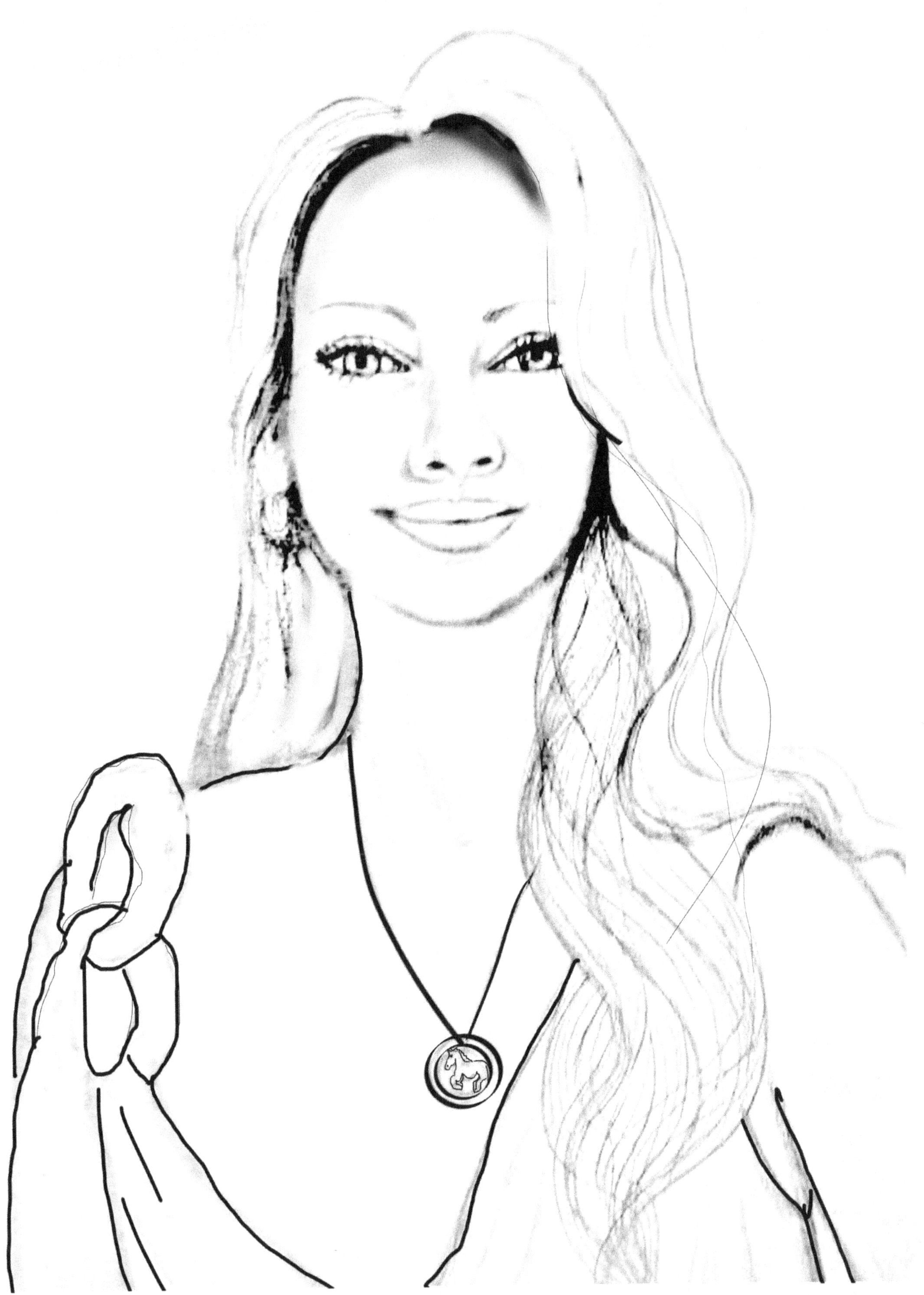